Responses to 101 Questions on God and Evolution

Other books
by John F. Haught
published by Paulist Press——

The Promise of Nature
What Is God?
What Is Religion?
Science and Religion

Responses to 101 Questions on God and Evolution

John F. Haught

PAULIST PRESS
New York, N.Y./Mahwah, N.J.

Cover design by Jim Brisson

Copyright © 2001 by John F. Haught

Library of Congress Cataloging-in-Publication Data

Haught, John F.
    Responses to 101 questions on God and evolution / John F. Haught.
        p.   cm.
    Includes bibliographical references.
    ISBN 0-8091-3989-8 (alk. paper)
    1. Evolution—Religious aspects—Christianity—Miscellanea. I. Title: Responses to one hundred one questions on God and evolution. II. Title: Responses to one hundred and one questions on God and evolution. III. Title.
BT712 .H385 2001
231.7′652—dc21

                                                                2001021368

Published by Paulist Press
997 Macarthur Boulevard
Mahwah, New Jersey 07430 USA

www.paulistpress.com

Printed and bound in the
United States of America

CONTENTS

II. *Darwin and Theology* (Questions 32–49)

III. *Creationism* (Questions 50–59)

INTRODUCTION

Evolution is still too recent—and surprising—an idea for the world's great religious traditions to have yet digested it fully. But increasingly, educated believers want to know how scientific pictures of life evolving connect with the content of their religious traditions. So far they have received very little guidance on this matter either from the classic sources of spiritual wisdom or from religious leaders today. The world's spiritual traditions originated long before science and long before Darwin, and so we cannot expect them to have addressed directly the questions his fascinating ideas have raised. Pope John Paul II's recent statement (1996) acknowledged the scientific evidence for evolution, but it offered very little in the way of theological reflection on the issues surrounding it. This lack of direction need not be lamented, but instead taken as an opportunity for the creative evolution of religious thought itself.

Probably nothing in contemporary science has proven more theologically provocative than the topic of biological evolution. Debates about the religious implications of Darwin's ideas have been going on for almost a century and a half, and they are as heated today as they have ever been. The present book is a contribution to this ongoing conversation. It will offer one theologian's response to some of the main religious questions surrounding evolutionary biology.

The questions included here come not only from experts who have thought deeply about evolution, but also from nonexperts whose acquaintance with evolution is casual and perhaps misinformed. The responses are those of a Roman Catholic theologian whose professional life has been devoted in great part to the study of issues in science and religion. The questions and responses are a somewhat selective compilation drawn from my contact over the years with lay audiences, students,

1

scientists, philosophers and theologians. They arise from religious believers as well as scientific skeptics, from those who embrace evolution and those who disdain the very idea, from scholars as well as the scientifically uneducated.

Although as a theologian I must address questions about evolution from the perspective of Christian tradition, I hope that my responses will be of such breadth as to be of some help to those of other religious persuasions also. I have arranged the material in a way that will allow me to introduce—along the way—the rudiments of what we might call a "theology of evolution." In these pages, of course, I can provide only hints of what such a theology would look like. For a more systematic and intensive discussion, interested readers may wish to consult my recent book *God After Darwin: A Theology of Evolution* (Boulder, Colo.: Westview Press, 2000).

Probably the most fruitful way to read the present work is to start at the beginning and follow the numerical ordering. However, at the risk of some occasional repetition, I have designed most of the responses in such a way that they can be read separately and in random sequence as well.

Finally, I hope that teachers of courses in science and religion, as well as adult education classes, will find the questions and answers offered here a helpful stimulus to further discussion. Because of constraints on verbosity—a 350–500-word limit for each question is editorially required in this series—each response can amount to little more than a taste of what obviously deserves much lengthier consideration. I trust then that readers will take the curt and candid way in which I address the questions as indicative of word-saving economy and not of any pretense to finality.

I.

DARWIN'S REVOLUTIONARY IDEA

1. Why has evolution been such a religiously troubling idea?

The idea of evolution as such is not necessarily disturbing to religious people. Awareness that things change cumulatively over time, and that life in some way "evolves," is an ancient one. Even St. Augustine allowed that beings on earth can emerge gradually from "seed principles" sown by the Creator in the beginning.

Rather, it is Charles Darwin's version of evolution that has been so shocking. Why so? Because (1) it offers a whole *new story of creation,* one that seems to conflict with the biblical accounts; (2) Darwin's notion of natural selection appears to diminish, if not eliminate, *the role of God* in creating the diverse forms of life; (3) Darwin's theory of human descent from "lower" forms of life appears to question age-old beliefs in *human uniqueness* and *ethical distinctiveness;* (4) his emphasis on the prominent role of *chance* in evolution seems to destroy the notion of *divine providence;* (5) Darwinian evolution seems to rob the universe of *purpose,* and human life of any permanent significance; (6) and, at least for many Christians, Darwin's account of human origins seems to conflict with the notion of *original sin,* of the "Fall," and therefore remove any need for a savior.

There is no denying that "evolution" has meant all of these things to a large group of Christians in America. To a vast number of them Darwinian "evolution" has ushered in many of the evils of the last century and a half. Religious voices sometimes claim that evolution is the source of moral relativism, Nazism, Communism, the breakdown of family life, the rise of sexual promiscuity, AIDS and numerous other ills. It is clear that for many people the implications of Darwin's work are broadly devastating.

Darwin's ideas came into the Western world, says Andrew Dickson White, "like a plough into an anthill." The religious and intellectual worlds of the nineteenth century were not prepared for Darwin and went scurrying this way and that. In all candor, I believe that even now, at the beginning of a new millennium, we are still reeling from the shock Darwin apparently delivered to many traditional beliefs. We continue to devise ways of ignoring or domesticating the rawness of his troubling picture of life. It may turn out, though, that an appreciation of Darwin's revolution can considerably deepen and widen our understanding of God.

2. Who was Charles Darwin?

Charles Robert Darwin (1809–1882) was born in Shrewsbury, England. His grandfather was the renowned Erasmus Darwin (1731–1802) who also had held evolutionary ideas. Darwin's mother died when he was only eight, and this loss was a major event in his life. He soon thereafter began attending a day school in which he developed a taste for collecting shells, coins, minerals, and so forth, a passion that later led to his interest in becoming a naturalist.

In 1818 Darwin enrolled in a boarding school very close to his home, and remained there until 1825 when he turned sixteen. He then entered Edinburgh University, where he found the lectures so boring that he took to solitary reading and long walks in the countryside. He attempted the study of medicine but found it distasteful. At the encouragement of his father he went on to Cambridge (1828–1831) with the intention of becoming a clergyman. Though not especially devout, Darwin fancied that the life of an Anglican country cleric would give him the opportunity to indulge his interest in nature.

Sometime during his Cambridge period he apparently read works by the famous theologian William Paley (1743–1805). Paley is famous for his "watchmaker" argument according to which the orderly arrangements in the physical world, like those of a watch, provide evidence of an intelligent maker. The remarkable way in which organisms are adapted to their environment provided not only Paley but most other religious thinkers at the time a sufficient reason to believe in a designing deity. It is important to know that Darwin was deeply impressed by this so-called "natural theology," with its argument that the "book of nature" could lead us to God no less surely than could the Bible itself. Later on, Darwin's theory of natural selection would lead him and countless others to reject Paley's argument.

As it turns out, Darwin's stay at Cambridge was, in his own words, "sadly wasted." And he goes on to say that "no pursuit at Cambridge was followed with nearly so much eagerness or gave me so much pleasure as collecting beetles." At Cambridge, however, he met a few good scientists and read several important books that stirred up in him "a burning zeal to add even the most humble contribution to the noble structure of Natural Science."

Soon after completing his studies at Cambridge, where he focused on geology, Darwin was granted the opportunity to accompany Captain Robert Fitzroy aboard HMS *Beagle,* a ship commissioned to survey the shoreline of South America. His five-year adventure on the *Beagle* (1831–1836) was to change not only Darwin's own life and thought, but eventually the life, beliefs and intellectual culture of much of the rest of the world as well.

3. What is Darwin's theory in a nutshell?

Darwin's theory is remarkably simple. It has two main facets: first, all forms of life descend by way of gradual modification over the course of time from a common ancestor; and second, the explanation of this gradual modification, including the emergence of new species, is *natural selection.* Natural selection means that those organisms most able to adapt to their environments will be "selected" by nature to survive and produce offspring, while nonadaptive (and therefore reproductively unsuccessful) organisms will perish. At first Darwin called his theory "descent with modification," but later on he accepted the label "evolution."

Before he could call evolution a scientific theory, Darwin had to find a "mechanism" to explain how the emergence of new species takes place over the course of time. In 1838 (more than twenty years before he published *On the Origin of Species*), while reading Thomas Malthus's *An Essay on the Principle of Population,* he suddenly found his answer. Malthus had noted that the growth in human population is always limited by the supply of food available, so there will always be a struggle among numerous offspring for the limited amount of sustenance. In this contest, nature will ruthlessly "select" the strong and eliminate the weak.

After reading Malthus, Darwin concluded that in *any* living species the struggle for existence will allow favorable variations to be preserved, while unfavorable (nonadaptive) ones will be eliminated. Within a population of finches, for example, those individuals accidentally endowed with beaks shaped to crush the kinds of seeds available in their habitat are more likely to survive than those not so lucky. And being able to survive, they will obviously have a better chance than other individuals of reproducing and passing on their better-adapted beaks by heredity to subsequent generations. Over a long period of time small adaptive changes can accumulate and bring about not only changes within a given species, but at times new and distinct species as well. Today evolutionists call the small changes within a species *microevolution,* and the larger changes that lead to new species *macroevolution.*

Curiously, once he arrived at his theory of natural selection around 1838, Darwin waited another twenty years before making it public. Only after he learned that a somewhat similar interpretation of evolution was about to be published by Alfred Russel Wallace did he rush to prepare an "abstract" of his own theory. This abstract took the form of the famously hefty monograph *On the Origin of Species.*

One reason Darwin took so long to put his ideas into print may have been his need, as a scientist, to be cautious. A good scientist does not bolt into the public arena until the evidence for a revolutionary new idea is as complete as practically possible. Darwin, no doubt, was a careful scientist. But another reason for the delay in publication may have been the reluctance of this temperamentally modest and unassertive man to introduce ideas that he must have known would have a religiously explosive impact.

4. Darwin and the Bible tell such different stories about the origin of species. Can they be reconciled?

Both scientific skeptics and religious believers often share the assumption that we have to choose *between* the two. "At least in the eyes of academics," the evolutionary philosopher Daniel Dennett writes, "science has won and religion has lost. Darwin's idea has banished the Book of Genesis to the limbo of quaint mythology." On the other hand, many religious readers of the Bible contend that Genesis refutes Darwin. Both sides assume that the Bible is somehow supposed to give us scientific information. However, Darwin's theory and the biblical notion of divine creation are really incomparable. One is deeply religious, the other scientific, so there can be no meaningful conflict.

Nevertheless, when it first appeared, Darwin's new "creation story" seemed, at least to many, to replace rather than complement the biblical narratives. England in Darwin's day was quite evangelical, as was America. Most devout people at the time took the biblical accounts of origins literally. The world was considered to be only around six thousand years old, and each living species was created separately, in a fixed way, by God in the beginning. Geologists had already begun to expose the temporal depth of the fossil record, but religious thinkers had found clever ways to reconcile the new findings with a literal interpretation of the Bible.

Darwin issued a shockingly new creation story, one that seemed quite impossible to map onto the venerable biblical narratives that had been so firmly imprinted on the sensibilities of generations. Even today, one of the challenges of Darwinian science to our religious understanding is that of how to hold together the story of creation by God and the story of evolution by natural selection. The so-called "creationists" (see below, questions 50–54) consider any such reconciliation impossible, and so they simply reject Darwin's story as inaccurate and even unscientific. Many evolutionists, on the other hand, dismiss the Bible as "myth" incompatible with science. How are we to settle this debate?

The most direct way is simply to acknowledge that the Bible is not science, and Darwinian science is not revelation. This advice was already implicit in Pope Leo XIII's encyclical *Providentissimus Deus* at the end of the nineteenth century. While discussing the question of how to interpret the scriptures, the pope admonished his readers not to look for scientific information in biblical texts. This simple instruction, were we to follow it consistently, could prevent an enormous amount of anguish and unnecessary confusion. The point is that we should never have placed Darwin's story into competition with biblical creation narratives in the first place.

By and large, Roman Catholics and other nonfundamentalist Christian churches have avoided this mistake, but major strands of fundamentalist and evangelical Protestantism continue to view the Bible as scientifically accurate. As a result they consider Darwin's science to be incompatible with biblical "truth."

5. Aren't there parallels between the biblical story of creation and the scientific story of evolution?

Some interpreters, especially the so-called "day-age" creationists, have tried to show that there is a parallelism between the Priestly account of the "days" of creation in Genesis 1:1-2:4a and the modern scientific understanding of the long "ages" or epochs in the history of cosmic evolution. In this interpretation, what the Priestly creation story refers to as a "day" (in the six "days" of creation) does not need to mean literally twenty-four hours, but may be taken metaphorically as an entire "age" in the context of natural evolution.

Attempts to make out this kind of parallelism between the Bible and science is sometimes called *concordism*. Whole books have been devoted to the concordist approach, and judging by their sales they have proved to be quite popular. Concordists want to avoid placing the Bible into unnecessary competition with scientific understanding. Hence, they look for ways in which biblical creation accounts will not come off as sounding too archaic to be taken seriously by the contemporary scientific mind-set.

In one recent version, that of scientist Gerald Schroeder *(God and The Big Bang),* the biblical notion of a "day" in Genesis can be taken literally if we appeal to Einstein's theory of relativity: the passage of time is experienced differently in distinct inertial frameworks. What seems to be billions of years when seen from one frame of reference may be only twenty-four hours when viewed from another. In this way, the biblical timing can apparently be brought into "concordance" with science.

The problem with concordism is that it is still biblically literalist at heart. It may sometimes be a looser kind of literalism than that of the hard-boiled creationists, but it remains obsessed with the same need to show that the Bible must somehow meet the standards of contemporary science in order to display its substance appropriately. In effect concordism makes the Bible into an obscurely premodern source of scientific information.

Concordism may allow a few scientifically-educated believers to cling to a rather literal reading of the biblical texts. But like creationism, it fails to dig beneath the literal meaning of religious texts in order to arrive at a level of depth where evolution and theology can be related to each other in a more substantive and exciting way.

6. What exactly are the main Darwinian challenges to the idea of God?

There are two: one relating to divine knowledge and power, and the other to God's love, justice and compassion.

First, Darwin taught that the relative differences in organisms' adaptability are accidents, in the sense of being undirected by any guiding intelligence. Some organisms "just happen" to be more "reproductively fit" than others. This randomness of variation suggests that we live in a makeshift universe, one devoid of design or intelligent governance. It therefore places in question our religious trust in divine providence.

Second, Darwin's ideas seem to dispute the notion of God's love, justice and compassion. The competitive struggle for survival between strong and weak organisms, or between the "fit" and the "unfit," offends our sense of compassion and fairness. The "law" of natural selection seems so blind and impersonal that theology after Darwin must show how it can be compatible with the notion of divine love and justice.

Thus evolution places in question both the providence and the goodness of God. While evolutionists cannot positively disprove the existence of God, many would claim that the cruelty of evolution fits more comfortably a godless universe than one rooted in divine power and love. Richard Dawkins, after noting how malevolent one form of life can be toward another, concludes: "The universe we observe has precisely the properties we should expect if there is, at bottom, no design, no purpose, no evil and no good, nothing but blind, pitiless, indifference."

It is worth noting, of course, that theology has always had to wrestle with the question of how suffering and evil can be reconciled with the twin themes of divine power and divine love. This is the timeless "theodicy" problem. So the main theological questions raised by Darwin are not entirely new. To many believers the Darwinian challenge to the notions of divine providence and compassion doesn't add much to the agonizing set of questions already on the table for theology. It seems to pale, for example, when placed alongside the history of human violence and suffering, and especially the brutalizations and exterminations during the last century.

And yet Darwin and his followers have exposed a ravine of suffering previously hidden from our view. Our new awareness of the immensely long story of life and its suffering prior to our own very recent evolutionary emergence adds new breadth to our perennial concern about God's permission of pain. Any wide-awake theology today cannot honorably ignore the immense scale that evolutionary science now gives to the intractable issue of innocent suffering.

7. What did Darwin himself think about God?

It is difficult to be certain. I am inclined to think of him as a somewhat reluctant agnostic, but there are varying opinions about his religious leanings, and especially about his beliefs at the end of his life.

After returning in 1836 from his famous sea voyage, Darwin spent the next twenty years brooding over his discoveries. In the Galapagos Archipelago six hundred miles west of Equador, he had carefully recorded how the finches there differed from island to island and from the mainland of South America. He was puzzled by the differences not only among the birds, but also among other groups of animals like iguanas and turtles. Having exhibited his drawings and specimens to expert naturalists back home, with their help he came to see that the differences were not merely variations within a single species, as he had supposed, but instead indications of distinct species.

At the start of his voyage Darwin had assumed, as did almost everyone else at the time, that all species had come into being by God's *special creation* in the beginning. He had also followed the tenets of William Paley's natural theology, an approach that argues for the existence of God on the basis of the adaptive design of living beings. But if special creation by God is the explanation of life's diversity, Darwin wondered, why are there so many varieties of finches (and other kinds of animals) instead of just one consistent type of each? If God is an intelligent designer, why has there been so much tinkering with the original designs? After extensive reading and consultation, Darwin began to doubt the traditional theological conviction that species had been "fixed" from the beginning of time, and he started to develop what came to be called his theory of "evolution."

Reflection on what he had observed during his sea voyage would eventually contribute to, but not necessarily be the main cause of, his doubts about the existence of God. It has been surmised that the death of his father and ten-year-old daughter may have been the main reasons for his growing religious skepticism.

In any case, Darwin did not see himself as the outright atheist that some modern writers have claimed him to be. And he was very reluctant to disturb the devout religious faith of his wife, Emma. In his autobiography he does pointedly state that "disbelief crept over me at a very slow rate, but was at last complete. The rate was so slow that I felt no distress, and have never since doubted for a single second that my conclusion was correct." Still, Darwin continued to refer occasionally to the work of a "Creator," or to a remote deity who created the universe and its general laws, but then pretty much left it on its own. Perhaps his beliefs can best be labelled "deistic."

8. Isn't evolution merely a "theory?"

Some religious people try to blunt the sharp edge of Darwin's ideas by denying that evolution is really scientific. They claim that Darwin's great idea is "only a theory" and that observation does not support it.

However, to say that evolution is "only a theory" and not "factual" betrays a serious misunderstanding of what "theory" and "fact" really mean in scientific work. A theory is a broad way of organizing and rendering intelligible the observable data uncovered by scientific exploration. And nothing becomes a scientific "fact" except in the context of an overarching theory. Theory is not something that dissolves or disappears once we get to the "facts." It abides as the intelligible context in which all facts are identified as such.

In the realm of science, therefore, it is never good form to say that something is "merely" a theory. A scientific theory is not just a wild guess spun out of thin air. And so, as far as evolution is concerned, to call it a theory does not diminish its scientific standing at all. Scientists have to situate all of their data and hypotheses within the general framework of some broad conceptual framework, such as Newton's or Einstein's *theories* of gravity, in order to make sense of nature at all.

The real question here, however, is whether the theory of evolution is supported by sufficient data. The answer to this question is undoubtedly yes but, like all other scientific ideas, evolutionary theory is always subject to improvement and revision. From a scientific point of view evolutionary theory has already firmly established itself by making good sense of numerous phenomena that would otherwise remain unintelligible. There is an abundant amount of data that supports the theory: for example, the fossil record, biogeographical distribution, comparative anatomy, geology, embryology, radiometric dating, and now the study of genetic timetables.

It would be difficult to explain the fossil record and other evolutionary data if we took the Bible literally and measured terrestrial events only in terms of a few thousand years rather than thousands of millions of years. On the other hand, evolutionary theory in combination with geological knowledge and other sciences now gives us a thoroughly reasonable account of life's history on earth. We can expect that evolutionary science will undergo refinement again and again, as all scientific theories do, but it is a strength of science, not a weakness, that it leaves its ideas open to such correction.

9. Has anybody ever actually observed evolution taking place?

Evolutionary changes have been observed in bacteria, finches' beaks, fruit flies and peppered moths. In the latter case scientists found that the number of white moths declined and dark ones multiplied when trees in England became covered with soot as a result of industrial pollution. The darker moths proved more adaptive because they could be camouflaged more easily on soot-blackened bark, and thus avoid being eaten by birds. Surviving in greater numbers, therefore, they understandably produced more offspring, and so their kind began to dominate. Once the trees began to return to their natural color, the white moths started to reappear.

But this kind of evolution, known as "microevolution," does not pose a problem for many religious opponents of Darwin. Even creationists allow for modification *within* a particular species. Perhaps the best example of intraspecies variation is the domestic dog, where differences can be extremely pronounced even where interbreeding is still possible. What creationists and other anti-Darwinians reject is "macroevolution," the process through which completely new species evolve.

According to evolutionary science, whether because of geographical isolation, gradual genetic drift away from a parent population, or other ways of diverging from their ancestors over the course of time, new species do emerge. This process, known as "speciation," brings about entirely new species which, except for occasional hybrid forms, scientists define in terms of their incapacity to interbreed.

However, opponents of evolution, especially biblical literalists, claim that since nobody has ever actually observed any really important speciation occurring, evolution is not empirically grounded. They insist that the idea of macroevolution is inadequately rooted in observation and therefore cannot qualify as good science. Science, they go on, must be able to reproduce results over and over experimentally, and evolutionary biology cannot do this in the case of speciation. One creationist, who helped draft the 1999 Kansas Board of Education's exemption of evolutionary science from the required secondary school curriculum, is reported to have said that evolution is a "lie" and a "deception" because "you can't go into the laboratory or the field and make the first fish."

Such a pinched understanding of how science works is obviously unacceptable to scientists. It is of course true that we humans don't live long enough to observe firsthand the speciation events that Darwin and his followers have found imprinted in the fossil record and more recently in the genomes of various species. But the shortness of our own life spans is not enough to lessen evolution's scientific standing.

None of us witnessed the Hawaiian Islands being formed, but few will doubt the scientists who theorize that volcanic activity caused their appearance over the course of many millions of years. Nor did we directly witness the big bang; yet big bang cosmology is as secure as most other scientific theories today. Likewise, evolutionary theory is in no way enfeebled by the fact that we have not directly observed speciation. We can reasonably infer its reality from the data presently available.

10. How reliable are Darwin's ideas considered today?

Today Darwin's theory, brought up to date by genetics, is stronger than ever in the scientific community. At the beginning of the twentieth century, Darwinian science at times seemed to lack the requisite evidence to be classified as scientifically reliable. Today, however, Darwinism is the central core of biological science. In fact, Darwinian evolution has now become the integrating concept in a number of other sciences as well. ( )

If it had not been for the discoveries of the Catholic monk, Gregor Mendel (1822–1884), however, Darwin's ideas would have had a much harder time of it. What was missing in Darwin's own theory was a clear understanding of heredity. He knew nothing about genes which we now understand to be the units of heredity. He had erroneously supposed that the features of organisms are shaped by a "blending" of parental characteristics in the blood. In 1866 Mendel demonstrated that the various features of organisms, such as the color of sweet pea blossoms, had to be transmitted by way of discrete units—what we now call "genes"—rather than by a mysterious mixing of parental traits.

Genetics has had the effect of supporting and refining Darwin's evolutionary theory. What Darwin referred to as random variations are now known to be undirected genetic *mutations*. By the 1940s Mendelian genetics had joined up with Darwin's theory in what Julian Huxley called the "Modern Synthesis," a theory known today as neo-Darwinism. (In responding to the questions in this book, unless otherwise indicated, I shall use the term *Darwinism* in such a way as to include neo-Darwinian developments.) Subsequently many biologists have thought of natural selection less in terms of individual or group survival, and more in terms of the survival of pools of genes. To some scientists evolution is essentially a matter of genes being selected to get into the next generation.

The science of genetics also backs up evolution by documenting the cellular and molecular similarities that point to life's common descent. Genetic studies indicate our kinship with all other forms of life. The human genome (our species' genetic endowment), for example, considerably overlaps that of other animals in the order of primates, and shares similarities even with bacteria. Along with comparative anatomy, embryology, paleontology, geology and other sciences, genetics has given us more indisputable evidence of evolution than ever.

11. Aren't there gaps in the fossil record that point to the special creation of each new species directly by God?

Such a question scarcely conceals an anxiety that unless God directly fashioned all the species of life, our sense of divine creativity will be impoverished. However, there is no good reason to think that the special or separate creation of each species by God, whether in the beginning or during the course of natural history, should be a reason for enlarging our appreciation of the Creator. Far more impressive would be a God who creates a universe opulently endowed with the capacity to give birth—from within itself—to many species during its own fruitful unfolding. It is no mark of piety or faith for us to require a God who could not possibly have allowed life to emerge in the spontaneous manner that evolutionary science has discovered.

However, to speak more directly to the question, many paleontologists have noted what seems to many of them to be "gaps" in the fossil record. The issue of gaps is vigorously disputed by scientists. But even if there are such gaps, is this a good reason to doubt the general validity of Darwin's science?

Darwin himself assumed that evolution was a very gradual process involving minute changes which, after accumulating over a long period of time, would occasionally bring about new and distinct species of life. In general this is what the fossil record shows to have happened. However, in some regions fewer transitional forms have turned up than the theory would seem to predict. There appear—at least to some scientists—to be "gaps" in the fossil record where we might have anticipated a less uneven distribution of forms. Not surprisingly, anti-Darwinians, especially creationists, have gained new confidence from these so-called gaps. The best way to account for the dearth of intermediate forms, they say, is the biblical notion of God's special creation of each distinct species of life.

However, there is no doubt among most biologists today that transitional forms abound, including many that fall between our primate ancestors and modern Homo sapiens. It is also important to note that only a very small number of bones ever become fossilized, and of these only a tiny fraction ever gets found by paleontologists. This alone explains some of the apparent gaps.

At the level of science itself, Niles Eldredge and Stephen Jay Gould have proposed a controversial theory known as "punctuated equilibrium" to explain the apparent gaps. In biological evolution long periods of "equilibrium" can go by, they hypothesize, without very much change. Occasionally, however, this equilibrium is "punctuated" by explosive transformations, such as occurred in the Cambrian period nearly six hundred million years ago. From afar this intense creativity may seem like "special creation." But when we look at it up close we observe that even the "punctuations" take up millions of years of gradual change.

Furthermore, as the Jesuit paleontologist Teilhard de Chardin wrote in *The Human Phenomenon,* the beginning of any new form of life will be so fragile and insubstantial that records of its appearance will inevitably be quickly erased. We should not expect, therefore, to find many transitional forms. Consequently, there is no reason to abandon the fundamental Darwinian paradigm. And the fossil record, even with all of its unevenness, should provide no comfort to antievolutionists.

12. If "special creation" is not required for bringing new species into existence, doesn't this render the whole idea of God superfluous?

According to almost all biologists today, cumulative genetic change over time can bring about new species without requiring any special miracles. Microevolution can gradually bring about macroevolution. That we do not directly witness speciation happening is due simply to the fact that we don't live long enough. The emergence of new species, after all, can take millions of years. The development of the whale from earlier land mammals, for example, is not directly observable, but it can be reasonably inferred from the trail of fossil evidence. For an idea to be truly scientific it does not have to base itself entirely on direct empirical discovery. Not any of us were able to observe the supernova explosion that preceded the birth of our galaxy, but scientists can justifiably conclude that there was one. So likewise with speciation.

Generally speaking, what marks off one species from another is an inability to interbreed. Usually for speciation to occur a small group of organisms must become isolated from a larger population for a vast period of time. Over the course of this time genetic variations in the smaller, isolated population will make much more difference than they would in a larger group. A daughter population will eventually diverge so far from its ancestral and sister branches that the sharing of genes among them becomes no longer possible. In this way new species can eventually emerge without the miracle of special divine intervention.

However, the absence of special creation or divine intervention in evolution does not mean that a deep and adequate explanation of life can dispense with the notion of God. In fact, the very depth of divine creativity is consistent with its working through more "natural" levels of causation such as the ones evolutionary biology studies. In any case, trying to locate God's activity within or at the level of natural biological causation really amounts to a shrinkage of God. This approach is known as "god-of-the-gaps" theology. It places divine explanation in the breaches of human inquiry instead of locating God's influence at a much more profound level, one that is inaccessible to science itself.

A god-of-the-gaps approach is a science-stopper, since it discourages scientists from digging deeper into the processes of nature. But, even worse, it is theologically idolatrous. It makes divine action one link in the world's chain of finite causes rather than the ultimate ground of all natural causes.

13. Is there clear evidence that we humans evolved from nonhuman primates?

Yes. The evidence is abundant, and it is only denied by those who have decided in advance that we humans simply *cannot* be closely linked genetically and historically to other species of life. Once again, of course, nobody has directly witnessed primates developing into humans, but the empirical markers for such evolution are sufficiently abundant. In fact, fossil evidence of the journey from primates to humans is more bounteous than it is for countless other evolutionary transitions.

That this question is repeatedly asked today—in spite of the clear evidence of our own biological evolution—is the sign of a deep underlying anxiety. Won't a vivid sense of our continuity with the animals undermine the common belief, endorsed by all traditional religions, that we humans are radically distinct from other living beings?

Such apprehension is hardly alleviated by recent information that we share over 98.4 percent of our genes with chimpanzees. However, we should not forget that it takes considerably less than one percent of our genes to make us enormously different from chimps. Genes, after all, contain *information,* and in the realm of information the tiniest quantitative variations can add up to the most massive qualitative differences. By changing just a few letters in this sentence I can alter my meaning drastically. Analogously, a relatively small percentage of overall genetic differences can lead to great differences when expressed phenotypically (that is, in the organism as whole). Consider, for example, how much the human brain differs from that of chimps.

Nevertheless, we should not forget the significant message of evolution that there is also continuity between humans and other animals. Today, especially for ecological reasons, it seems appropriate to reflect on our close kinship with other forms of life. We may now fruitfully recall that we are a species among other species, many of which we are now destroying—often perhaps because we have overemphasized our discontinuity with other kinds of life. It is no affront to our self-esteem to learn that we are part of a complex community of life-forms. In fact, the accounts in Genesis already anticipate the need to recognize our continuity as well as discontinuity with the rest of life.

An important question, however, is at what point in the evolution of our species did true humans actually appear? Is there any place in the fossil record over the last four million years or so where we can say that we clearly see the arrival of fellow humans? Were the now extinct Neanderthals truly human? What about *homo erectus* or *australopithecus?*

Some would argue that primates became human when the line between mere consciousness on the one hand and *reflective* self-consciousness on the other was crossed. But we will never know when this occurred. Others would cite the invention of language, or laughter, but it is impossible to find hard records of any of these transitions.

Philosopher Hans Jonas argues that a line was crossed very sharply, and in a way that is more archeologically visible, when our ancestors began to create the *tool,* the *image* and, above all, the *grave.* We have very solid monuments of these phenomena, and they all signal a radical innovation in the story of life on our planet.

14. What significance do ancient tools, images and graves have for understanding our place in evolution?

Making tools, painting images and preparing graves are all indicative of a new kind of existence in primate evolution, one that was able to transcend a purely instinctual style of life.

In making tools, for example, what is significant is that the act of creating the tool is distinct, and quite often very distant, from the act of actually using it. (Here I am drawing on ideas of Hans Jonas.) Tool-making implies a capacity to stretch one's consciousness forward into the future, to anticipate actions far removed from the present moment. Chimps sometimes use stones, and birds occasionally employ sticks, as "tools" to insert in the holes of trees to get at ants or grubs. But they are tool-*users* more than tool-*makers.* They do not first retreat to a remote place, days ahead of actual use, where they work in a focused way sharpening their stones and sticks, preparing them for later employment. Early humans, on the other hand, had to spend a considerable amount of time fashioning stones into axes, for example. And they did this at a time and spatial distance quite removed from the occasion of actually using them. No axes or spearheads adorn the groves where animals have gathered.

Second, images sketched in caves many thousands of years ago record a kind of awareness unlike anything that occurs in the gestures of earlier fauna. Painting the semblance of an animal on a cave wall (e.g., at Lascaux in France) and then garnishing it with figures of arrows is possible only in a kind of thoughtfulness that functions at a spatial and temporal remoteness from the actual hunt. In our early human ancestors, at least by 40,000 years ago, nature was beginning to transcend itself in an entirely new way.

Finally, our capacity to transcend ourselves so dramatically is nowhere more vividly or poignantly evident than in the adornments surrounding the gravesites of early humans. Careful preparations that preceded the burial of family members, and the ritual of burial itself, indicate a radical departure from the past.

In our ancestors' preparing of the grave and the body for burial, perhaps we can make out the earliest sparks of what would eventually flame out into the religions of the world. In the earliest manufacturing of tools we see the first stirring of what would evolve into technology. And in the earliest images lie the promise of many forms of aesthetic creativity that enliven and give meaning to our lives today. In the tool, the image and the grave nature is already evolving into culture. And once culture emerges, the blind laws of biological evolution are no longer in complete control of the life story on earth.

15. Is evolution still going on? If so, what will happen to our species in the future?

There is no good reason to think that the general laws of nature have now been suspended. Natural selection will continue to work with remorseless consistency wherever it can. But now that human culture has appeared, evolution takes on a whole new character. Because of the invention of culture the pressures of natural selection are less intense, and in some instances eliminated.

As far as nonhuman life is concerned, one of the environmental factors it has had to adapt to is the ever burgeoning prominence of our own species on this planet. Already innumerable species have disappeared because they were unable to adapt to our often predatory presence.

At the same time, viruses like AIDS, which are not very good at making copies of themselves, can rapidly mutate into types that survive our most potent medicines. This is an example of life adapting to us. And if you want an even clearer example of how evolution still goes on, you can literally watch bacteria at this very moment changing with great rapidity into forms that resist our best antibiotics.

What specific directions human evolution will take in the future is quite unpredictable. After we humans emerged we invented culture, thus changing the whole way in which our own species adapts to inhospitable environments. Endowed with intelligence, language, creativity, ethical sensitivity, religious longing, and eventually scientific knowledge and technology, we learned to survive many threats that nature poses. The character of evolution changed radically when it moved from nature to culture. Culture adapts us to nature in a manner that diminishes the role of chance and blind selection operative prior to our appearance. Now perhaps the dominant threat to our survival is not nature but ourselves.

Still, if we follow the patterns of cosmic evolution, we can observe that occasionally major leaps in complexity have occurred, and we may expect them to occur again in the future. Atoms gave rise to complex molecules, molecules to infinitely more complex cells, and cells to higher organisms. Teilhard de Chardin has pointed out that, generally speaking, the evolutionary rise in physiological complexity has been accompanied by a corresponding rise in the intensity of consciousness. Matter has become increasingly "spiritualized." Why shouldn't this trend toward the building of mind and spirit continue on into the future?

In us humans evolution has now become conscious of itself. We have the freedom to choose or reject opportunities to carry the evolutionary adventure into a new future. The fact that we don't always seem to be making much headway—and indeed often seem to be regressing—is not sufficient reason for discouragement. Remember that in comparison with geological or evolutionary measures of duration we have been on this planet only a flash of time. Perhaps evolution has the potential to unfold in surprising ways that we can hardly anticipate at the present.

Along with Teilhard, however, I believe that the inspiration of religion is indispensable for this to happen. Only the spirit of charity, animated by "a great hope held in common," can sustain evolutionary process at the level of human existence.

16. Could life have originated by chance?

Darwin vaguely speculated that life first appeared accidentally in a "warm little pond." Today evolutionists conjecture that the building blocks of self-replicating life began to come together by an improbable series of accidents about 3.8 billion years ago.

Such a proposal may initially seem completely hostile to faith's ageless conviction that God is the author of life. However, there is no necessary conflict at all. In fact, it does not diminish God's providential role at all if the natural world is so extravagantly gifted that, at relevant moments in its unfolding, random events open the door abruptly to a creativity that gushes forth in astonishingly new and unpredictable ways.

Scientists have discovered that carbon compounds, the chemical building blocks of life, are abundant in outer space. Formerly experts had routinely considered the universe to be essentially hostile to life. Life, it was said, had precious little chance of ever coming about, and that it did so at all is a most unparalleled fluke. Of course, a good number of scientists still think this way, but an increasing number of them now suspect that the universe is put together in such a way that life is almost inevitable. Given the "vital dust" (carbon compounds) that biologist Christian du Duve finds so abundant in interstellar space, it would be most surprising if life never emerged. Some astrophysicists today emphasize that from its opening moments ours has been a universe bursting to break forth into life—at least eventually.

If the universe is so charged with potential for life, then the actual moment of life's eruption is not so momentous as it would be if matter were inherently inimical to life. The emergence of life may well have been a "random" occurrence (or series of occurrences), in the sense of not being explicitly "directed" by a supernatural agency. The emergence of the first instance of life can be thought of as welling up from the earth's and the universe's own bountiful potential. It is more appropriate to conceive of God as the ultimate depth and ground of nature's resourcefulness than as a magical intruder.

Theology, therefore, does not need to deny that there was an element of randomness in the first appearance of life, as well as in the mutations that occur later in evolution. It is unseemly to picture a divine "designer" stitching atoms and molecules together in a special act of "design" in order to make the first living cell. Rather, we should think of the universe, in Howard Van Till's words, as "richly endowed" in a comprehensive way for giving birth eventually to life from within its own inner storehouse of creativity.

So the emergence of life, and later of human intelligence, can be pictured more like the sudden budding or blossoming of a flower, embryonically present from the start, rather than something grafted on from outside. We are still far from understanding the details of this marvelous emergence. But we must avoid introducing a "god-of-the-gaps" that would discourage further scientific illumination of the fascinating events involved in the origin of life.

17. Doesn't evolution lower our dignity by blurring the distinctions among matter, life and human persons?

It may seem so at first, but careful reflection will show that no such danger exists. However, let us first see why evolution gives this impression.

Traditionally the thinking of the West (as well as much of the rest of the world) has clung to a hierarchical cosmology. By "hierarchical" I mean that the universe was organized vertically into a "Great Chain of Being" running from lifeless matter at the lowest level, through plants, animals and humans to God at the highest level.

Evolutionary ideas, however, seem to have toppled the cosmic hierarchy around which our cultural, intellectual and ethical life had been organized for centuries. If evolution is true, are there any sharp breaks between humans and the rest of life? Further, doesn't evolution make mindless matter, not God, the author of all things? Don't life and mind emerge only gradually in the cosmic drama, apparently by accident, out of a universe that is fundamentally lifeless and mindless?

According to scientific accounts, after the first primitive form of life had appeared, biological evolution began. Very slowly more complex kinds of life descended from the first living cells. Predecessors of today's millions of species of plants and animals began to proliferate from a common material ancestry. Eventually beings with limbs, nervous systems, and minds emerged out of the mud. Then over the last several million years brains grew in size and cognitive capacity. At some point life became human. Humans in turn produced ideas about the good and about God.

This is not the story that classical religion and hierarchical cosmologists were prepared to hear. Is it any wonder, then, that not only biblical literalists, but also sophisticated proponents of hierarchical theology (sometimes called the "perennial philosophy") have repudiated Darwinism? The evolutionary story of life evolving from matter seems to destroy the hierarchical structure in which almost all classical literature, art, ethics, law, politics and theology had been sited.

Evolution looks at things chronologically or historically rather than vertically. From this horizontal perspective, lifeless and mindless matter seems to be the author of all. No sharp lines separate matter from life, or life from mind. Historically and scientifically speaking, everything appears to fade into everything else. Recent developments in molecular biology and genetics only seem to confirm the impression that matter, life and mind merge into one another on a seamless continuum of atoms.

If there are no sharp breaks in this evolutionary story, the hierarchical sense of discontinuity that formerly separated matter from life, and life from mind, seems to get blurred out in the seamless flow of the evolutionary river. The question then arises whether any basis exists for the timeless assumption by religions and cultures that life is "higher" than matter, or that mind, spirit or soul even exist at all.

I believe it can be shown that a revised version of the hierarchical view is consistent with the evolutionary data. But you can see here why it is that evolution raises theological questions even beyond the scare it gives to biblical literalists.

18. How, then, can you have a religious-hierarchical sense of reality without rejecting evolutionary science?

In evolution, nature's hierarchy is an *emergent* one (one that arises gradually over time), and so it cannot be understood in purely vertical and static terms. But even after Darwin, we can still clearly distinguish among various levels and values of being. We can preserve both evolutionary science and hierarchical discontinuities simply by recognizing the role of *information* in living beings.

Here, I think, contemporary science itself can be of help to us. For some time now scientists have been registering the fact that nature is not just a continuum of matter and energy. Rather, nature is composed of matter plus energy plus *information*. Perhaps a brief look at the way information "works" in relation to the matter-energy continuum can help us understand how nature can be both evolutionary and hierarchical at the same time.

Hierarchy entails discontinuity between one level and the next. And it is *informational patterning* that introduces the discontinuity. The presence of distinct informational patterns can organize the world into discontinuous hierarchical "levels" without causing any suspension of the physical and chemical processes in which the information is encoded. The information resident in DNA, for example, can shape life without violating any laws of chemistry.

To clarify this point, let me use a very simple analogy (adapted from Michael Polanyi). The page you are now reading is a good example of a hierarchical structure. There are (at least) three "levels" here. The "lowest level" of the hierarchy consists of the chemical laws that make ink bond with paper. Then there is an intermediate level that consists of words, grammar, letters of the alphabet, and so forth. And, finally, there is a third and "higher level" consisting of the specific content I am communicating by arranging words, letters, grammar, and the like to form a specific informational pattern or meaning on the page. What I want to emphasize is that in communicating the specific content you are now reading on this page I am not violating or disturbing the "lower levels." I don't need to violate alphabetical, grammatical or lexicographical rules to write what I'm writing here. Nor do I disturb the chemical laws that make black ink bond with the white paper. Instead I rely on all of these.

Chemistry—to stick only with the lowest level here—may be able to say a lot about how ink bonds with paper, but it is not equipped to read any "higher level" meanings that might be present on this page. Likewise, evolutionary science might be able to describe the physical and chemical events involved in biological phenomena without being able to discern the deeper meanings in life to which religions seek to awaken us.

The point is that *informational discontinuity at one level can exist side by side with physical continuity at another.* The quiet presence of information can bring about hierarchical discontinuity in evolution without in any way disturbing the continuity at the levels of biological or chemical processes. So it is simply illogical to conclude that evolutionary science reduces life and mind to lifeless physical stuff. Information makes all the difference in the world, though it does so in a very quiet, unobtrusive way.

19. Doesn't evolution rule out the existence of a distinctively human soul?

Christian hope, we must first recall, looks toward the resurrection of the body and not the immortality of a soul that can be finally separated from the material world. The notion that we are composed of soul and body is sometimes interpreted in such a way as to make us humans look like alien spirits temporarily imprisoned in material bodies, waiting for death to release us to our true home "up above." But it is difficult to map this ancient (and rather platonic) anthropology onto the new evolutionary picture of life. Perhaps, then, Darwinian science compels us now to reconsider what we mean by the "soul."

Instead of eliminating the notion of a human soul in order to make us humans fit seamlessly into the rest of nature, perhaps it would be wiser to acknowledge that there is something analogous to "soul" in all living beings. We humans have souls, of course, but in its own way so does every other living being. Here it is helpful to remember that the term "soul" is our English translation of the Latin *anima,* from which the word "animal" is derived. Soul has always meant an "animating principle," and so everything alive must in some way be "ensouled."

For centuries religious thinkers, including St. Thomas Aquinas, have been comfortable with this more democratic distribution of an animating principle throughout the domain of life. Aquinas spoke of a vegetative and animal soul along with the human. It was especially after Descartes (1596–1650) and the rise of mechanistic views of nature that people began to suspect that other living beings are soulless.

But even in a scientific age it is not too speculative to attribute an interior aspect to each living being. Maybe all living organisms have an aspect of "subjectivity" hidden from scientific objectification. In each of us this interiority would be associated with a distinctively human soul. But other living beings may possess a hidden "subjectivity"—widely varying in the degree of experiential awareness—where they are intimately touched by and participate in the divine Spirit whom we may refer to as Life-Itself.

Once we allow for this broader understanding of soul, we may interpret evolution as the momentous story of soul-emergence. Evolution is the adventure of life gradually becoming more conscious, centered, free and capable of love—but also capable of great evil. This understanding allows us to move beyond the artifice of thinking that God abruptly "injects" prefabricated "souls" into our species or into our bodies at certain artificially defined points in evolution or embryogenesis. Instead we may understand the Spirit of God as present in *all of life,* animating each species in a manner proportionate to its characteristic mode of organic or informational complexity.

The emergence of the human soul, then, would not be a glaring exception to this animating process, but instead a most intense exemplification of a general aspect of creation and evolution. This interpretation also leaves open the possibility of analogous developments in life elsewhere in the universe.

20.   The Bible claims that we are made "in the image and likeness of God." Doesn't evolution contradict this idea?

There are two ways to look at evolution's implications for our own sense of spiritual identity and worth. One way is to interpret evolution as dragging us down into the realm of beasts who live without ethics and culture. In this view Darwin may seem to be the bearer of bad news to many strict moralists. On the other hand, we may read the story of our evolutionary emergence in such a way that it allows us, now as never before, to envision the rest of life as sharing—at least in some way—in the dignity bestowed on us by the Creator.

As far as we know, however, we are the only species on earth endowed with freedom, responsibility, and the capacity to love selflessly. (We may observe a kind of "altruism" in other species, but their apparent selflessness flows from instinctual endowment rather than freedom.) Our biblical ancestors' intuition of a uniquely human set of characteristics, therefore, clearly justifies a religious anthropology that attributes a great nobility to our species. It is especially in our capacity for making and keeping promises, and for compassionate love, that we can say that we are made in the image and likeness of God.

But does this mean that other creatures do not also bear the imprint of their Creator? After Darwin, we are challenged to see ourselves as falling within the context of a more protracted life-story and a wider life-community than we were ever aware of before. As an organic unity, this wider community of life reflects the Source of Life in a richer way than any species, including our own, does all by itself. We are learning that it is part of the very definition of human existence that we are interdependent with the rest of life. In this sense evolutionary science has been a great gift to religious thought, not to mention ecological spirituality. It has widened our sense of what it is to be human by filling in our natural prehistory. And it has enlarged and enriched our self-understanding without demanding that we distance ourselves completely from other creatures.

It is especially in its capacity for intense interrelationship that the organic world as a whole bears the imprint of its Creator. God, after all, is distinct from the world not by being unrelated to the world, but by being the most intimately related Being of all (as implied in the Christian doctrine of the Trinity). Our own bearing of the image and likeness of God, therefore, also means our having the capacity for intense relationship. We show forth God's image and likeness not by separating ourselves from the wider circle of life on earth, but by intensifying our relationship to it. Evolution helps us to understand and appreciate this communion. If anything, it supports rather than undermines the biblical sense of our being created in God's image and likeness.

21. What are the implications of evolution for morality?

Both Darwin's theory of common descent and that of natural selection raise questions about human morality. If all forms of life descend over time from a common ancestor, aren't we much closer to monkeys than to angels? And if we are part of the animal kingdom, we may forgivably ask: What is there to keep us from behaving like our nonhuman kin? Furthermore, if life has so far advanced only at the expense of the weak, why shouldn't we humans accept "survival of the fittest" as normative for our own relationships with other humans as well as with other species?

In response to these interpretations of Darwin, two points can be made. First, justifying human conduct by appealing to the way biological evolution works is an instance of what the philosopher G. E. Moore has called the "naturalistic fallacy." This is the attempt to define what is humanly good in terms of some "natural" aspect of the world. The fallacy consists of a logically illicit leap from what "is" in the world to what "ought to be" in the realm of human ethics. Even during Darwin's own lifetime the philosopher Herbert Spencer infamously attempted to derive an ethic from what he was the first to call the "survival of the fittest." And, especially in America, an experiment known as "social Darwinism" salved the consciences of some of our wealthiest tycoons who interpreted their colossal acquisitiveness as consistent with the law of selection. Today we can see more clearly that such a justification is based not only on moral ruthlessness, but also on logical delusion.

The second (and related) point is that human morality (along with religion) belongs to the realm of "culture" which is distinct from nature. Human culture is a "world of meaning" radically different from anything we find in the rest of the animate world. Of course it is quite "natural" for humans to invent culture, but the specific meanings that make up culture cannot be derived simply from a study of nature. The birth of culture was a whole new stage in the cosmic story, and one that cannot be adequately interpreted in terms of the natural sciences.

What we see going on in human culture, as theologian Gerd Theissen has noted, is a reduction of the pressures of natural selection. Our social institutions, laws, customs and religions often—though not always—protect the weak rather than facilitate their elimination. The "unfit" begin to have a chance at survival also. By the time the ancient biblical prophets came along, humans had begun to develop the sense of a God who is preferentially disposed toward the poorest and most disadvantaged. Clearly religions would unanimously agree that Darwinian ideas alone cannot provide an adequate basis for morality.

22. Some evolutionists think that Darwinian evolution can provide a good explanation for our ethical and religious tendencies. On what basis do they make this claim?

Today this claim is associated especially with the Harvard biologist E. O. Wilson and his followers. Wilson is the inventor of "sociobiology," an attempt to explain human behavior in terms of the Darwinian notion of reproductive fitness. Wilson believes that biology has powerfully explained the features, or "design," in all other living beings through the notion of "adaptation." So why shouldn't biologists try now to account for all of our human characteristics in terms of reproductive fitness also?

The general problem they have to solve is how to make Darwinian sense of altruism. By "altruism" biologists understand any behavior, whether in the realm of animals or humans, by which an organism sacrifices its genetic future for the sake of other organisms, usually those related to it. If evolution is about competing and struggling for survival, then why do some organisms (or persons) instinctively sacrifice themselves and thus leave no offspring. And doesn't the widespread ideal of altruism in human life place us completely beyond the sphere of evolutionary biology?

According to sociobiology, our relatively new awareness of how genes work in evolution allows us to extend Darwinian explanation even into the realm of human ethics and religion. Genetically nuanced biology was not available to Herbert Spencer and the early social Darwinists, so their intuition that evolution sets norms for human behavior could only be put forth in a primitive way. But today some biologists understand evolution not so much in terms of the selection of individuals or populations as the selection of pools of genes. This genetic perspective allows for a more "inclusive" understanding of reproductive fitness and one that, at least to sociobiologists, allows us to make scientific sense of ethics and religion.

"Inclusive fitness" is a notion first developed by the late biologist William Hamilton. It means that we should attribute the notion of fitness—in the sense of reproductive success—not so much to individuals or populations of organisms as to certain arrays of genes distributed throughout a group of organisms. This wider notion of fitness allows that certain altruistic organisms will be more vulnerable to extinction than others. But even though the altruists in a population may die before reproducing, their self-sacrificial actions may actually enhance the genetic fitness of the larger group. The genetic endowment of the whole group is "selected" to survive, even if certain individuals perish.

The usual example is that of the prairie dog who warns its close relatives that a predator is nearby, but by sticking its neck out too far in making the warning gets eaten by the predator. This particular individual does not survive, but its "sacrificial" gesture, by warning other prairie dogs to get back into their holes, allows the genes of its kin to survive into subsequent generations. Thus its altruism serves the cause of "inclusive" fitness.

Isn't it likely, the sociobiologists now ask, that humans—or better, human genes—have invented morality and religion to improve their own inclusive fitness? If we look at fitness from a genes-eye perspective, altruistic or self-sacrificing behavior—by which I might diminish my own personal reproductive opportunities—can improve the reproductive fitness of my fellows. If I lay down my life for my friends, or if I decide to live celibately and generously like Mother Teresa, my own genes may not find their way into the next generation; but the genes of those whose lives my charity has improved will get passed on, including genetic traits that make some of us altruistic. My moral and religious commitments will in this way have contributed to the inclusive fitness of my species. So Darwinian explanation seems to be able to account even for ethical and religious behavior.

23. What response can theology give to this sociobiological "explanation" of morality and religion?

It may begin with an appeal to logic. The attempt to give a purely evolutionist explanation of morality and religion is an instance of the "genetic fallacy." The genetic fallacy is the illogical assumption that we can adequately understand a phenomenon if we know how it originated. It is called a fallacy because it ignores the possibility that over the course of time development and transformation can take place. The question of how moral virtues and religious beliefs came about in the first place is logically distinct from the question of whether they are true or false.

The sociobiologist claims that ethics and religion "came about" as adaptive phenomena—that is, they originated to serve the cause of the need of human genes to survive. Therefore, they must not be true. The ideas of goodness and of God, according to E. O. Wilson and some of his disciples, were made up by our ancestors in order to allow them to feel at home in an unfriendly universe. Feeling at home, their genes were better able to survive, but the content of the ethics and religions our ancestors have devised is itself pure illusion.

How are we to respond to this position? Let us concede that ethics and religion have served the cause of evolutionary adaptation—although just how they have done so is considerably more convoluted than socio-biologists have typically thought. Even so, it is illogical to jump from biological explanation of the origins of religious ideas to judgments that these ideas are illusory. The fallacy employed here is one that assumes that if a specific trait is biologically functional it must therefore be untrue.

Theology may simply reply to the sociobiologist that if a compassionate God does actually exist it would be very surprising if our religious attempts to understand or worship this God turned out to be biologically nonadaptive. The practice of ethics and religion would have to be at least consistent with the character of living processes—in this case the rules of gene survival. If religions and ethical systems caused our genes to die out, obviously they could not survive either. But this does not make gene survival an adequate explanation of morality and religion.

Even though human altruism and religion, like all other forms of life, emerged in the course of an evolutionary process and therefore have some continuity with their evolutionary ancestry, their ethical and cognitive status must be assessed on grounds other than those of their evolutionary prehistory. In any historical development the original stage can become increasingly insignificant. To evaluate something simply on the basis of its historical origin is the "genetic fallacy."

So, for example, the science of chemistry is said to have developed historically out of the medieval practice of alchemy; and modern astronomy is said to have its origins in ancient astrology. But over time chemistry has abandoned everything in alchemy except a general interest in material change; and astronomy now preserves from astrology only a passionate interest in the heavens. In both cases the historical origins have become inconsequential. If we followed the genetic fallacy, however, we would have to reject contemporary chemistry and astronomy because of the lowliness of their historical precedents.

Sociobiology and evolutionary psychology can be taken seriously by theology as long as their practitioners are humble enough to confess that neo-Darwinian theories about the biological origins of ethics and religion cannot give us an *adequate* understanding of these phenomena, let alone tell us whether they are in touch with reality. Unfortunately, I have found that it is rarely the case that proponents of sociobiological interpretation are willing to make such reservations in the interest of logic and methodological modesty.

24. Since there are serious disagreements among neo-Darwinians, shouldn't theology avoid commenting on evolution until all the facts are in?

It is true that at times there are bitter disputes among biologists, especially regarding exactly how evolution takes place. Some evolutionists, for example, think that almost every feature of living organisms plays, or at some time in the past has played, a purely adaptive role.

Others, however, allow that there are characteristics in living beings that just happen accidentally to be there, with no adaptive function at all.

Additionally, there is disagreement among Darwinians on what the primary unit of selection is in evolution. Is it simply individual organisms? Is it groups or populations? Or is it perhaps pools of genes? These and many other issues, for example the role of sex in selection, are still matters of considerable debate.

However, in spite of such disagreement, almost all biologists agree on those features of evolution that are going to be of interest to theology. These are the elements of chance, natural selection and time. Most biologists take for granted that evolution requires a great excess of random—in the sense of undirected—events. These "contingent" occurrences can range from the genetic mutations that take place in the cell, to asteroid impacts such as the one that may have wiped out the dinosaurs sixty-five million years ago. The point is that many events in the story of life seem to be contingent. That is, they seem to occur purely by "chance," making us suspect that nature is largely unplanned and undirected. Where is God in all of this?

Second, most evolutionists share the assumption that natural selection is blind and impersonal, a fact that raises serious questions about how to think of divine providence in such an apparently uncaring world.

And, finally, evolutionary biologists, whatever their differences may be, agree that evolution requires long periods of time. This temporally extravagant aspect of evolution makes us wonder why a divine, infinitely intelligent Creator would "fool around" for billions of years before bringing about living beings. Why not create everything at once and get it over with?

So, even though biologists may differ on the details, they generally agree on the three fundamental features of evolution that theology must wonder about today: chance, natural selection and massive amounts of time. No matter what version of evolutionary biology you follow, the same fundamental questions arise—so there is no need for theology to keep waiting for a tighter scientific consensus before commenting on the new story of life.

A theology of evolution must ask what sort of religious sense we can make of the randomness, impersonality and cruelty of natural selection, and the fact that life seems to have appeared only gradually, over a period that science now estimates to be 3.8 billion years. What kind of a God would preside over such a messy, prolonged and serendipitous process? Theology cannot and should not postpone the task of addressing these questions. (Subsequent questions in this book will attempt to deal with them.)

25. Why do so many educated people today still have such a hard time reconciling evolution with religious faith?

Perhaps it is not always evolutionary science as such, but the materialist philosophy in which it is sometimes packaged, that makes evolution seem so forbidding. Sometimes prominent evolutionists proudly parade Darwinian ideas as *inherently* materialistic and atheistic. William Provine of Cornell University, for example, insists that today a biologist cannot be a religious believer without sacrificing honesty and truthfulness because one cannot be a good biologist without being a materialist.

Scientific skeptics generally assume that evolutionary science requires a materialist interpretation of nature. Materialism (or "physicalism") is the belief that matter, the purely physical realm, is all there is to reality. Materialism goes hand in hand with *scientism,* the belief that science is the only reliable road to truth. And when scientism and materialism are combined with biology, evolution gives the appearance of being inherently atheistic. Richard Dawkins, a renowned British biologist, declares that Darwin has given atheism its firmest intellectual foundation ever. And today some of Darwin's devoted followers insist that atheism is the natural context for Darwin's "dangerous idea." If educated people can make such claims, then other educated people may be inclined to go along.

Meanwhile, many conservative Christians, including some well-educated ones, also agree that evolution logically entails atheism. Most theologians in the Roman Catholic and mainline Protestant traditions, along with the majority of Jewish religious scholars, claim to have no theological difficulties accepting evolutionary biology. Even so, they often wonder what possible theological significance evolution might have.

Many biologists unnecessarily present the theory of evolution already so snugly wrapped up in the blanket of materialism that they cannot imagine how it could ever be reconciled with religion. At the same time, biblical literalists insist that the Bible provides the most authoritative *scientific* account of life's origin, and that true believers must reject evolutionary ideas, a claim that continues to arouse the bitter hostility of the scientific community. The impasse between scientific materialists and biblical literalists tends to dominate public discussion of evolution.

Meanwhile other, less simplistic, ways in which scientists and theologians have integrated evolutionary science into religious thought, enlarging the concept of God in the process, get very little notice in the popular press. Many educated people have simply not been exposed to such alternatives. In my opinion the blame for this goes in great measure to seminaries and schools of theology which, generally speaking, do a poor job preparing ministers and religious instructors to meet the intellectual and spiritual needs of the scientifically educated.

26. Isn't the personal God of the Bible too small to accommodate our new evolutionary picture of life and the universe?

The astronomer Harlow Shapely remarked one time that science has displaced "the anthropomorphic, one-planet Deity" of biblical religion. And the idea of a personal God such as we have in the Bible is a stumbling block for many evolutionary scientists as well. As evolutionary biology and cosmology have widened the temporal and spatial dimensions of nature, the biblical portraits of God may no longer seem to have kept pace. To many scientific thinkers what we have traditionally called "God" now appears too small for them. This is perhaps why some scientists have turned to Eastern religious philosophies and other forms of mysticism to satisfy their very human craving for infinite horizons.

In any case theology must take pains to ensure that our notion of God is not slighter than the epic of cosmic and biological evolution itself. Many of us pick up our impressions of God when we're very young, and even though we grow up and our minds expand, our understanding of God often fails to grow along with us. For many scientists and other educated people the sense of a "personal" God gets lost in the increasingly magnified immensities of time and space. It becomes difficult for them to participate in traditional forms of worship because "God" seems much less imposing than the cosmos. Many scientists lose interest in religion not out of laziness or ill will, but because religious educators, pastors and preachers fail to represent God in terms proportionate to the new evolutionary portraits of nature.

One could make a forceful argument here that our schools of theology and seminaries need to do much more by way of educating their students to connect the worlds of religion and science. This has not taken place very often, and such neglect has impoverished theology and religious life. Theologians have generally abandoned consideration of the universe in modern times, thinking it sufficient to deal with human, social, political and historical issues. I have encountered a number of scientists, though, who are looking earnestly for a religious framework large enough to contextualize their scientific knowledge, but who only rarely find it in conventional ecclesiastical circles or the suburban pulpit. Likewise many students pass through college without ever being challenged to connect what they learn about the universe in science classes with a proportionate religious awareness.

A coherent theology, however, need not worry that an appropriate sense of the majesty of God will ever be overtaken by science. For no matter how large science discovers the cosmos to be, it will still be small in comparison with the infinite depths that genuine religion associates with the divine. The larger our sense of the cosmos is, in fact, the better sense should we have of the dimensions of deity. Religious believers, therefore, must never be afraid to learn from science about the immensity of the universe. Scientific knowledge, properly understood, can only enlarge our sense of God.

27. How can I hold onto my faith in God while studying evolutionary biology?

I personally know many excellent biologists who are quite comfortable with evolutionary *science,* who can consistently sort out the scientific information that supports Darwin's theory from any materialist or atheistic agenda, and who are quite comfortable with good theology. In my own work I meet such individuals on a routine basis. If you're looking for a famous example of such a scientist let me just mention the name of the geneticist Theodosius Dobzhansky, one of the founding figures of the modern synthesis now known as neo-Darwinism, and also a devout Christian. Another example is my friend Ken Miller—a biologist at Brown University, a Roman Catholic, author of widely-used biology textbooks and a very helpful recent work called *Finding Darwin's God.*

Briefly, I think there are two general ways in which you can hold together evolutionary science and religious faith. An easy way is to keep your religious life and inner thoughts about God completely separate from, and "uncontaminated" by, your evolutionary knowledge. I do not personally recommend this approach, but I know that many scientists and theologians are comfortable with it. We may call it simply the "separatist" approach. It insists that science itself has nothing to say about values, about meaning or about God. So we should keep everything we learn in science completely locked up in a compartment of our consciousness isolated from our religious convictions.

The appeal of separatism is at times irresistible. As long as we keep our questions about evolution sealed off in one area of our mind, and our questions about God in another, there will be no occasion for conflict. Accordingly, we can go about our scientific business without having to raise troubling questions about God, and our religious business without worrying about whether Darwinism has theological implications.

The other approach—let us call it "engagement"—cannot honestly separate science, especially evolutionary theory, so cleanly from religion. Since truth cannot contradict itself, scientific and religious truth must be reconcilable. However, the engagement approach acknowledges that after Darwin we simply cannot have the same thoughts about religious faith as we may have had before. After Darwin the whole creation and the entire story of life look different. So also do a lot of other things: human existence, morality, culture and, above all, God. According to the engagement approach, evolution does not require that we abandon faith and theology, but it does demand that these undergo a kind of development of their own.

There is no danger to religious faith or theology in opening itself to such transformation. In fact, such growth helps to keep faith and theology alive and healthy. And if we take the time to think about God in terms of evolution, I believe that our religious understanding will have everything to gain and nothing to lose. As the believer approaches the Darwinian world it may be worth contemplating a simple but powerful instruction of the French philosopher and mystic Simone Weil: "Christ likes us to prefer truth to him, because, before being Christ, he is truth. If one turns aside from him to go to the truth, one will not go far before falling into his arms."

28. The "separatist" response makes good sense to me. Can you say more about it and why you find it inadequate?

I can understand why some scientists, theologians and many others are content with it. Separatism helpfully allows its proponents to distinguish clearly between science and religion. It is especially effective in preventing the kind of confusion of science and belief that occurs in scientific creationism and scientific materialist interpretations of evolution. Advocates of the separatist approach claim that it actually keeps their religion and theology from becoming irrelevant. Since science is always changing, they say, theology runs the risk of becoming obsolete if it ties its formulations too closely to the science of any particular age. This occurred early in the modern period when some Christian theologians got too cozy with mechanistic understandings of nature. Maybe it will happen again if we allow theology to get too close to Darwin.

However, I believe that by insulating theology from contemporary science, and especially evolutionary biology, the separatist approach in effect isolates the very idea of God from God's own creation. It says in effect that no matter what we find out about nature, it won't have any real impact on our sense of God. Surely, though, if evolutionary science is at least approximately representative of the way life occurs on our planet, then theology must take it into account when it tries to understand and express what "God" means. Even if evolutionary theory will undergo more improvement or revision in the future, theology cannot just avert its eyes from the honest and impartial discoveries of biology, geology and paleontology. To do so, I believe, actually runs contrary to the incarnational thrust of Christian faith. After all, the biblical authors did not try to separate the sense of God from their own cosmological assumptions. Neither should we suppress our own best understanding of nature when we think about God.

The separatist approach still holds evolution at arm's length. It merely tolerates Darwin's science at a time when theology should be able to celebrate it. If we think carefully about evolution, I am convinced that it will considerably expand and deepen our understanding of God. (See especially questions 32 and following.)

29. How have the churches reacted to Darwin?

The churches' reactions have varied considerably from one denomination to another. Although Darwin clearly disturbed the faith of many church officials, even in his own time the idea of evolution was a theological stimulus to at least some of them. The popular Anglican churchman Charles Kingsley, for example, suggested that a creation unfolding gradually from primal forms points us to a more noble concept of the Creator than would a nonevolving world. His theology of evolution was reminiscent of ideas first expressed by St. Augustine (354–430) that in the beginning God "seeded" the creation with potential to give rise gradually to many kinds of beings over the course of time. Kingsley also thought that evolution allows us to think of God as more deeply involved in nature than previous scientific thought had allowed.

What about the Catholic reaction? In comparison with the animosity toward Darwin so prevalent among some other Christian denominations, Catholicism, on the whole, has been relatively hospitable toward Darwin's new science. There was strong resistance in the beginning, but for some time now Catholic theologians and church officials have had no serious difficulties with the topic of evolution, though it is still somewhat marginal to the everyday concerns of most of them.

Fundamentalist and much evangelical Protestantism, however, has found evolution especially offensive. About forty percent of American Christians still think evolutionary theory is inconsistent with belief in God, and their church leaders often officially support this opinion. The evolutionary picture of nature obviously conflicts with the literalist reading of scripture that many Christians still espouse. And the idea of our descent from more primitive forms of life seems to contradict the doctrine of our special creation "in the image and likeness of God."

Much of the ambiguity expressed in the various denominational reactions to Darwin can be explained by the fact that scientists themselves have often presented evolution as inherently atheistic. For example, as early as 1877 Karl Marx and Ernst Haeckel, both proponents of different forms of materialism—the doctrine that "matter" is all there is—had already enthusiastically endorsed Darwin's ideas. Some of the early papal opposition to evolution can be accounted for by the frequent association of the term *Darwinism* with philosophical materialism.

However, most of the churches' resistance to evolution can be explained simply by the persistence of biblical literalism in seminaries and other media of ministerial and religious formation. Until questions of biblical hermeneutics (how to interpret biblical texts) are resolved in favor of a nonliteralist approach to preaching and theology, we can expect evolution to remain a problem for many believers.

30. What have the popes taught about evolution?

A letter of Pius IX in 1877 expressed the suspicion that Darwinism is a "mask of science" behind which there lurks a purely materialist vision of nature. It is not surprising that whenever the idea of evolution has been closely linked to the philosophy of materialism church leaders in the late nineteenth and twentieth centuries, including popes, remained somewhat hostile to the Darwinian revolution. It did not help matters that the idea of evolution became associated also with "social Darwinism," the belief that in human social life the strong and wealthy have nature's endorsement, no matter how many others lose out in the struggle for success.

Pope Pius XII, in his encyclical *Humani Generis* (1950), granted that the human body may have evolved naturally over a period of time, but he insisted that God creates each human soul directly. For the most part Catholic scientists have found the pope's concession to be a liberating one. However, philosophers and theologians today often find the notion that the soul is specially and immediately infused into a human body to be a somewhat awkward formulation. (See question 19 above.)

As is now well known, Pope John Paul II in a statement issued in 1996 agreed that the evidence for biological evolution is convincing. Earlier papal documents sometimes condemned evolution, while others granted it lukewarm acceptance. Pope John Paul II's statement, however, decisively revokes previous misgivings about evolutionary science, and it implicitly encourages the development of an evolutionary theology. This is a major readjustment in papal teaching. (It is one of many instances we could cite of evolutionary change in papal teaching itself from one age to the next.)

In speaking of the papacy and evolution, it is instructive to remember that the issue of religious faith's compatibility with evolutionary science revolves in great measure around the question of how literally or metaphorically to interpret the scriptures. If you take Genesis literally, as though it were giving you a scientifically accurate depiction of the origins of life, you will have a hard time reconciling evolution and the idea of God. In his encyclical *Providentissimus Deus* (1893), Pope Leo XIII officially delivered Catholics of such an impossible undertaking by his simple instruction that we should not look for scientific information in the pages of scripture. Such caution serves to protect sacred texts from the trivializing that occurs whenever we put them on an equal footing with scientific treatises.

In 1981, some years before his more recent declaration on evolution, Pope John Paul II similarly rejected creationist literalism in an address to the Pontifical Academy of Sciences: "The Bible itself speaks to us of the origin of the universe and its make-up, not in order to provide us with a scientific treatise but in order to state the correct relationships of man with God and with the universe. Sacred scripture wishes simply to declare that the world was created by God, and in order to teach this truth it expresses itself in the terms of the cosmology in use at the time of the writer...."

31. What is the significance of Pope John Paul II's more recent message on evolution?

In 1996 Pope John Paul II went far beyond former papal tentativeness and formally agreed that the biological evidence for evolution is compelling. This remarkable adjustment has not met with unanimous approval among Christians—especially in the United States—many of whom continue to think of evolution as irreconcilable with the biblical accounts of origins. The pope, however, has simply given an official endorsement of the view long held by Catholic scientists and theologians that evolution is not contrary to Christian faith. This is a significant, if somewhat belated, development in the tumultuous story of evolutionary science and its relationship to religion.

Additionally Pope John Paul II's message is very sensitive to the fact that today some prominent evolutionists present their science to the public as though it were ineradicably atheistic. Unfortunately, celebrated evolutionists still often write about evolution as though in order to embrace it we must first commit ourselves to a materialist—and therefore atheistic—view of nature.

The pope's message allows that we may embrace the scientific evidence for evolution without feeling compelled to swallow the one-dimensional materialist literalism which, beginning in the nineteenth century, has consistently dogged the idea of life's descent. While Catholic theology has always held that there can be no real conflict between genuine science and faith, it does acknowledge that "scientific materialism" is irreconcilable with belief in God. Scientific method is one thing, but the materialist ideology in which scientific ideas are often packaged is another. Thus, before theology can appropriate evolution it has to unpack the clear scientific evidence and throw away the outer materialist and mechanistic wrappings that have so often unnecessarily enshrouded it.

In John Paul II's statement we may detect an underlying concern to avoid the merging of evolutionary science with mechanistic philosophies that interpret life as essentially valueless and meaningless. Once it has been delivered from materialist ideology, the cumulative scientific evolutionary evidence readily lends itself to a lively religious construal. Some contemporary Christian theologians even argue that the only kind of natural world consistent with the existence of the infinite love we call God is an evolutionary one.

Perhaps the most significant implication of the pope's message is that it revokes definitively a dark history of Vatican suppression of numerous modern theological efforts, especially that of Teilhard de Chardin, that had assimilated an evolutionary vision of life and the universe. Writings of numerous theologians had been held under suspicion, nominally perhaps for many other reasons, but in fact for their endorsement of a vision of evolutionary transformation that would also entail ongoing change in the church and lively development of its doctrine as well. Even today it is not so much the complexities of Darwin's theory, but the elementary fact that evolution means "cumulative change over time" that constitutes the largest barrier to acceptance among some church officials. The pope's message on evolution, I believe, officially revokes any basis for such resistance.

II.

_____

Darwin and Theology

32. Has Catholic theology been deeply influenced by evolutionary biology?

Catholic theology has generally attempted to be at least consistent with contemporary evolutionary science, but this does not mean that it has always been deeply influenced by it. In the last half of the twentieth century the synthesis of Christianity and evolution undertaken by the Jesuit paleontologist Teilhard de Chardin (1881–1955) has had some impact. And recently a few Catholic theologians have drawn upon non-Catholic religious thought, including the so-called "process theology" associated with the philosophers Alfred North Whitehead and Charles Hartshorne whose ideas are deeply evolutionary.

Emphasizing the doctrine that God's creativity works continuously, and not merely "in the beginning," Catholic theology allows for the possibility that evolution implies ongoing divine creation. It has firmly rejected all forms of fundamentalist "creationism," arguing that evolutionary science (as distinct from evolutionist materialism) is completely compatible with the doctrine of divine creation. It also holds that biblical revelation is debased whenever it is treated as a source of information that science can discover by itself.

Nevertheless, it seems accurate to report that Catholic theology today, along with Christian theology in general, is still not deeply touched by evolutionary ideas. Recent Catholic theology has been mainly preoccupied with issues relating to human history, freedom, personal spirituality, and social justice. Theological reflection on nature is still marginal in Catholic theology, and almost completely absent in the seminaries. In spite of Catholicism's strong sacramental tradition of relating divine activity closely to the natural world, its theologians now generally focus on God's activity in the human sphere rather than in nature and its evolution.

Fortunately, a slowly increasing number of Catholic theologians, especially women, are now objecting to this one-sided emphasis on human history at the expense of the cosmos. They claim that thinking about God only in terms of human concerns will only end up separating us humans further from the natural world that has given birth to us. They are beginning to reflect on the themes of revelation, incarnation and redemption in terms of cosmic evolution and not simply of human existence. This in turn allows them to articulate the ecological connections that bond our species with all of the other forms of life in a single "earth community." They are most grateful to Darwin and his followers for helping us deepen our understanding of our relationship to the natural world and its Creator.

33. What significance does evolution have for theology today?

First, evolution has forced some religious thinkers to broaden what is called natural theology. And second, it compels systematic theology to pay more attention to what we might call the "promise" of nature.

Natural theology—which looks for imprints of a divine creator in nature (usually some kind of "design")—is more inclined these days, as a result of Darwin's critique of William Paley, to look for signs of divine intelligence in the *whole cosmic picture,* rather than concentrating on the minutiae of insects' wings or fishes' eyes. Especially as a result of recent developments in the physics of the early universe, some advocates of natural theology are now entranced by the exquisite order they think must have been present in the initial physical conditions and fundamental physical constants of a life-bearing universe. Natural theology today, therefore, is often inclined to look for signs of divine influence in cosmic beginnings rather than in the adaptive fit of organisms to their environments.

Darwin's thought, however, also invites systematic theology to consider the fact that we live in an unfinished universe. Evolution means that creation is still occurring, as much today as in the beginning. The fact that the evolving universe and its life-story are still unfinished opens up the future to us in a refreshing and liberating way that previous pictures of nature did not allow. An unfinished creation invites theology to extend our hope not just to a heaven for humans hereafter, but ahead to a destiny that must somehow include the whole universe. This wider view of things also allows us to feel more forcefully that our own efforts, however insignificant they may seem at the moment, may nonetheless contribute to the great work of ongoing cosmic creation. It would be a pity if theology today failed to take advantage of all this good news implied in evolution.

Some theologians are also bringing out the ecological implications of our new awareness of living in a world-in-the-making. Stewardship in such a universe means more than just caring for what has been present from the beginning. It also means that we should nurture the process of creation so as to enable it to realize its inherent evolutionary potential for future unfolding. Believers can assume that the Creator of this universe has a vision for it that goes far beyond human powers of calculation. If so, then our destruction of life systems on earth today is a sinful strangling of the world's future evolutionary promise. It is of special importance for theology, in this respect, to take evolution seriously.

34. What do you mean by a "theology of evolution?"

A theology of evolution is a systematic set of reflections that tries to show how evolution, including those features that scientific skeptics consider to be incompatible with religious faith, illuminate the revolutionary image of God given to Christian faith.

A theology of evolution is not obliged to defend the emaciated notion of God that skeptics consider to be defunct after Darwin. It does not try to protect the remote "designing deity" that writers like Richard Dawkins and Daniel Dennett have in mind when they argue that evolution is inherently atheistic. A theology of evolution does not allow either creationists or scientific skeptics to define the meaning of "God," but instead takes as normative the sense of God given to us in the biblical experience.

Evolutionary biology now provokes theology to set forth in sharper relief than ever the biblically-based image of God as the compassionate and promising One who gives the divine self unreservedly to the cosmos. After Darwin we may still think of God as powerfully effective in the world, but we need to define more carefully what we mean by divine "power." We can still confess that God is Creator, active in the world and faithfully redemptive. But a theology of evolution will do so in a way that takes the data of evolutionary science fully into account.

Simply stated, the God of Christian faith is not one who overpowers the world and forces it to conform to a rigid plan. Instead God wills that the world "become itself" as fully as possible. This means that the world must be allowed the space and time to wander about, experimenting with various possibilities. While the mind of God is the source of all the alternative possible paths the universe may travel on its evolutionary adventure, we can safely suppose that a God of love would not compel it to follow a prefabricated itinerary unyieldingly. If God loves the world, then we can assume that God concedes to the world a certain degree of freedom to experiment with an array of possibilities in its becoming.

A theology of evolution will allow that evolution is by nature experimental, and that the cosmos and life must have some room to "wander about." The fact that we live in an expanding universe is itself indicative of the Creator's desire that the world have spatial and temporal latitude for experiments in emergent independence. A God who truly loves the world is intimately related to it, but in a way that allows the world to remain forever distinct from God. The process of evolution is the story of the universe trying out various ways of becoming distinctively itself. Divine power, therefore, is manifested as loving self restraint, as a "letting be" that permits the world to emerge as something other than God.

35. How does evolution change our understanding of God?

An evolutionary perspective, in the first place, proposes a massive shift in our understanding of where to locate the divine transcendence. God, we may now haltingly assert, is not exclusively "up above," but also "up ahead." Karl Rahner has put it that God is the Absolute Future. Reflection on evolutionary *process* has helped theology retrieve a deeply biblical sense of God as One who relates to the world as a giver of promises yet to be realized. God comes into this unfinished world from the future and creates it anew from out of the future. An evolutionary theology thinks of God and God's promise in terms of the "futurity" of being, rather than in terms of an eternal and immobile presence hovering "up above." This, however, is not so much a qualitative change in our understanding of God as a radical recovery of forgotten biblical insights about ultimate reality.

Second, the epic of evolution expands our sense of God by making us realize that divine care embraces the destiny of the whole cosmos. Hence we can no longer plausibly separate our own private aspirations from the fate of the entire creation. As long as religions believed in a static universe, perhaps human hope could understandably take the form of looking towards a rather individualist destiny in another world completely apart from this one. This "optimism of withdrawal," as Teilhard de Chardin calls it, dominated Western spirituality for centuries. Evolution, however, tells us that we are linked to the larger universe and a grand story of life in a prolonged process of becoming. The fresh new sense of our "togetherness" with this cosmos provides our hope with a broad new horizon. Evolution gives to our lives a stronger sense than ever of our being participants in the ongoing process of a *cosmic* creation story.

Finally, evolution has added a new accent to what we call divine grace. Divine grace allows for a "contingent" universe, one that is not shaped by deterministic necessity. In such a world, chance or accidents can occur. Theology should not have been surprised, but should have expected, that the created world would be open to the kind of contingency and randomness we find in life's evolution. St. Thomas Aquinas himself had argued that a universe totally dominated by necessity would not be distinct from God. The world has to have elements of nonnecessity or contingency in order to be a world at all. "It would be contrary to the nature of Providence and to the perfection of the world," he said, "if nothing happened by chance."

Only an independent cosmos could dialogue or be truly intimate with God. From this point of view, therefore, the epic of evolution is the story of the emerging independence and autonomy of a world awakening in the presence of God's grace. And divine grace, as Karl Rahner also often emphasized, makes the world more autonomous, not less. In the presence of God, the universe does not dissolve into nothingness or into God, but becomes a world distinct from its Creator. Evolution, therefore, allows us to feel deeply the primordial biblical conviction that God is gracious, liberating Love.

36. Why didn't God finish the work of creating the universe once and for all, in the beginning, billions of years ago?

The idea of an instantaneously complete creation, as Teilhard de Chardin says, is theologically unthinkable. A fully-created universe, one that failed to unfold gradually, would be only an extension of God's own being; it would not be a world unto itself. It would have no internal self-coherence, no intrinsic autonomy. Instead it would be a purely passive implementation of the divine will. It would be a frozen universe, one without a future and one incapable of supporting life since, by definition, living beings must continually transcend (go beyond) themselves to be alive at all. Temporal duration is an essential aspect of any creation that gives rise to life.

It is important for theology to realize that creation is still going on. The universe at this very moment is still in the process of being created. This awareness opens up the future ahead of us in a way that a static universe would not allow. And it reshapes our hopes so as to include not just our own personal survival of death but also the destiny of the whole universe to which evolutionary science links us.

Traditional theology spoke of three modes of creation: original creation *(creatio originalis),* continuous creation *(creatio continua)* and final or new creation *(creatio nova).* The concept of continuous creation portrays God's creative action as not just an event "in the beginning" but as an ongoing process. This "divine concursus" has long been part of Christian teaching, but one of the great gifts of post-Darwinian thought is that it makes the notion of ongoing creation much more immediate and understandable than at any other time in the history of Christianity.

In an evolving world creation happens every moment. It is even possible for us to say that the so-called "big bang" is not an especially privileged moment in the exercise of God's creative power. God's creative sway, as evolutionary biology makes evident, is being exercised just as much today as at the moment of cosmic origins. In other words, the big bang happens every day, and each day is, in a sense, still the dawn of creation. As Teilhard de Chardin put it, "Incessantly even if imperceptibly, the world is constantly emerging a little farther above nothingness." Evolutionary awareness allows us literally to feel the power of creation occurring in the here and now.

37. Doesn't the self-creativity of evolution diminish the role of divine creativity?

Scientific skeptics and biblical literalists would probably answer "yes." But in fact evolution's spontaneously self-creative character allows us to attribute creativity to God in a deeper way than before.

Prior to the scientific age, in the biblical period for example, everything that happened in nature seemed to be the direct action of God. Immediately behind the dawning of a new day, the occurrence of night, seasonal changes, floods, famines and the like, lurked the finger of God. In a prescientific age, when there was still no clear distinction between primary and secondary causes, it is not surprising that people portrayed God's action in this way.

However, after biblical religion made contact with Greek philosophy, and more recently with modern science, theologians had to concede that many events, such as the movement of the planets, changes in the weather, and eventually the evolution of life by natural selection, belong to the realm of secondary causes. We no longer look for unmediated divine manipulation in those events that seem to occur as the result of spontaneous natural processes. Today science seems to have gone even a step further in its disclosure of the "autopoietic" (self-creative) way in which many processes in nature unfold.

But the fact that nature is in some sense self-creative is not a denial of God's creativity. God's role as the ground of being, to use Paul Tillich's profound terminology, is immediately operative in the depths of all natural processes. To place God's creativity on the same plane as natural creativity is actually a demotion of divinity. The Spirit of God is hiddenly present in all instances of new creation. God's creativity is not remote and distant in the deistic sense of the Clockmaker who simply winds up world and lets it tick away on its own. God is most intimately involved in all that goes on in nature. But we need not imagine this creative presence in terms of our crude notions of efficient or mechanical causation. The creative Spirit of God "works" in a much more subtle manner, one that uses rather than manipulates or replaces natural processes.

There is no question, however, that many Christian apologists prefer the idea of an immediate "special creation" by God—one that *substitutes* for natural processes—when it comes to explaining the various designs, marvels and species of life. That evolution by natural selection can be creative seems contrary to their faith in a creative God.

But couldn't one argue that a creator who brings about a self-creating world, a world in which natural processes are themselves channels through which life and its evolution occur, is much more exalted than a creator who insisted on producing everything directly and without the mediation of creatures?

38. Why do you claim that a "special creation" of each species would actually diminish God's status as Creator?

It is now evident to science that many aspects of nature, and not just natural selection, are inherently self-creative. The big bang, the formation of galaxies, the cooking up of carbon and other heavy chemical elements in massive stars, the many kinds of chemical processes that occur in living beings, and life itself—these are all self-creative in one way or another.

Today science can testify also to the spontaneous creativity in nonliving complex systems and "chaotic" processes. The idea of self-organizing systems is now almost commonplace in scientific descriptions of nature. Here theology needs to pay close attention to what science has observed.

This means that when life came along in the unfolding of the universe it jumped astride nature's habitual self-organizing physical and chemical routines. So, in a broad sense, the creativity of biological evolution is no more of a challenge to the notion of a creator than are all the other instances of cosmic creativity. What theology must reflect on, therefore, is not only biological evolution's spontaneous creativity, but also the self-creative tendencies present in physical reality as such.

It is interesting to recall here that for many centuries prior to the birth of modern science religious thinkers had no difficulty believing in the spontaneous creativity of physical reality. Today we may smile at the medieval belief that piles of dung could generate maggots and flies, or that heaps of grain could give birth to rodents, but there was at least an acknowledgment that creation can be spontaneously creative. Ironically, it was especially after the birth of modern science in the seventeenth century that the realm of "matter" came to be thought of as so passive— and so alien to life—that the need for "special creation" of life by God became more intellectually appealing. Today's creationists, who claim to be defending ancient teachings, are often implicitly upholding a very modern set of beliefs about the inert character of matter. Fortunately science itself is now returning—in a new way of course—to an awareness of nature's spontaneity that got lost in the modern period.

In any case, a creator who calls a self-organizing and self-creative world into being seems much more deserving of our worship than one who insists on making everything directly, without involving creatures themselves. Therefore, to insist on special creation, as many Christians do, is to shrink God to the role of a magician. It is also a refusal to acknowledge the creative vocation that all creatures have in some degree, and which we humans have in a very special way. A robust theology of creation finds more to admire in a divine creator who calls this self-creating universe into being, than a "designer" who directly forces everything into a prefabricated blueprint.

39. Why would God allow evolution to bring about so many millions of kinds of living beings?

We can address the question of life's diversity at the level of both science and theology. At the level of science, Darwin provided an elegant and simple explanation of life's diversity. He assumed that all living beings have a remote common ancestry. Picture a tree hanging upside down, where all the branches and twigs emanate from a common trunk. As you move down the trunk you will see that many branches form over the course of time, but they all remain connected to the same trunk and a common root system. This was Darwin's famous tree of evolution.

Like any analogy this one only partially succeeds. For unlike, say, a cedar tree where all the branches look alike, on each branch of the tree of life you will find the proliferation of numerous twigs that differ markedly from those on other branches. We humans, for example, belong to a shoot known as the order of primates, and recent evolutionary scientists have reason to believe that the nearest ancestor we share with other extant primates goes back about six to eight million years.

The cause of all the branching on this tree, according to Darwin, is "natural selection." Natural selection of adaptive characteristics is the mechanism that explains how all the diverse forms of life came into existence over an immense amount of time. Working like a sieve, nature has filtered out and discarded all variations of life that have not been reproductively fit. Today, we realize that genetic drift may also cause evolutionary change, but natural selection (perhaps along with sexual selection) is still considered to be the fundamental agent of creativity in the biosphere, the realm of living beings.

With his extremely simple theory of natural selection, Darwin answered numerous questions that had been building up for centuries. In conjunction with developments in geology and some other branches of biology, his theory was able to respond elegantly to the question of life's diversity. And it also responded efficiently to such questions as why we find sharks' teeth and other marine fossils high up in the mountains, or why fossilized remains of animals in the lower levels of the geological record are generally less complex than those higher up.

Theologically, we can assume that the dynamism and diversity of life is indicative of the extravagance of divine creativity, which always remains discontent with the monotony of the status quo. Furthermore, as St. Thomas Aquinas argued, the infinite God can never be fully represented by any one creature. Hence God (continually) creates a multiplicity of beings so that what is lacking in one thing as far as representing God's infinite perfection is concerned can be supplied by something else, and that by yet something else, and so on. Only an awareness of the indefinite diversity of beings can lead us to an exuberant sense of the infinite.

40. Doesn't science make enough sense of evolutionary diversity all by itself? Why bring in the idea of divine creativity at all?

Nature is a book that we may "read" on many different levels. Theology professes to read beneath the scientific impressions of nature. In the depths of nature it discerns a dimension of divine creativity that works unremittingly without having to contradict scientific explanations of life's diversity.

However, today some scientific experts dogmatically insist that a scientific reading of nature (typically through the lens of their own specialty) is the deepest we can go in our human efforts to understand the creativity in evolution. For example, Richard Dawkins says that all that is *really* going on in evolution is the flow of genes striving to get into the next generation. This is enough to explain all of life's manifestations.

The only way to get beyond such literalism is to learn to read things on different levels. However, the testimony of all religions is that learning to read in depth requires a personal transformation, a radical change of heart as well as mind. Moving beyond literalism, whether it be biblical or scientific, requires from us a personal renunciation of the absolutist will to clarity and certitude.

There is a similarity between biblical literalism and what I am calling scientific literalism. Both are intolerant of ambiguity and insist on reading at only one level. They share an obsession with fitting their respective worlds into tight little packets where nothing overflows into uncertainty. In many ways, therefore, the whole set of issues we are talking about in this book is comparable to a reading problem. It is a problem of how to move beyond the literalism that sometimes takes over in both religion and science. Evolution, however, provides us a great opportunity to move both science and religion beyond literalism. Both nature and the Bible can be read, after Darwin, at deeper levels than before.

The literalist is one who denies that there are many levels of understanding and explanation, and who remains personally immune to the adventure of breaking away from the surface of nature or sacred texts. The literalist lives in what Edwin Abbott called *Flatland,* an allegorical world in which two-dimensional beings cannot conceive of the possibility of a third dimension, and who prosecute those who claim to do so.

It is our own attachment to Flatland that leads us to an *either/or* rather than a *both/and* way of thinking about natural and divine creativity. Thus we think we have to make a choice *between* explaining the diversity of life in terms *either* of natural selection *or* divine creation. Only a sense that there can be a "hierarchy of explanations" will allow us to realize that we are not forced into such a narrow option.

41. What exactly do you mean by a "hierarchy of explanations," and how can it help reconcile theology with evolutionary accounts of life?

Let me begin with an analogy. Suppose someone is driving your car down the street. You ask: "Why is my car moving?" At one level of explanation a good answer is "because the wheels are turning." At another level an equally acceptable explanation is that internal combustion has set the pistons, drive-shaft, and so forth, in motion. At still another level the answer may be "because Jim is driving it." And at another level the explanation might be "because Jim has to go to the store."

This is a simple example of a hierarchy of explanations. All of these explanations make sense *at their own level.* And all can coexist without contradicting or competing with one another. Taken together they constitute a richer explanation than any provides by itself.

Life in this universe also lends itself to such a hierarchy of explanations. Take cellular DNA, for example, one of the richest instances of complex design we can find in nature. How can we explain DNA?

DNA can be understood quite well at the level of chemistry. At another level, DNA can be understood by the geneticist in terms of its hereditary properties, features that don't interest chemistry as such. And, at a still higher level, DNA can also be interpreted by the Darwinian biologist as the fundamental unit of natural selection. Each of these levels can enrich our understanding of life. The evolutionist, moreover, does not have to be an expert in the "lower" levels (for example, biochemistry) in order to understand the role DNA survival plays in the origin of species. There is a legitimate autonomy in each of the sciences.

The famous Harvard biologist Ernst Mayr accepts the idea of a hierarchy of explanations. However, he claims that Darwin gives us the "ultimate" explanation of life. Mayr is not a theist, so he has no use for theology. He feels no need to look any higher in the hierarchy of explanations than the Darwinian notion of natural selection in order to find the deepest explanation of life. Similarly Richard Dawkins of Oxford University accepts in principle the notion of a hierarchy of explanations. But he abruptly declares that gene-survival is *all* that is going on when evolution brings about complex instances of design. Any allegedly "higher" or deeper level of explanation is superfluous.

However, theology has every right to suspect that both Mayr and Dawkins are still living in Flatland. For theology can also legitimately claim a place, at another level of the hierarchy, in the explanation of life. To do so it does not intrude—in a competitive fashion—into the various levels of scientific explanation, as though it has a "better" explanation than they do. Rather, theology claims that the *ultimate* explanation of evolution is divine creativity. And it does so without in any way disturbing the integrity of the various sciences.

In the case of the moving car, the fact that Jim wants to go to the store is a "higher" level explanation, but it does not contradict or compete with the other levels of explanation. Theologically speaking, the fact that God wants the universe to unfold in an extravagantly creative way does not abolish the chemical, genetic and evolutionary accounts of life.

42. In a specifically theological reading, what can we say is *really* going on in evolution?

Christian faith reflects on this question in the light of its own image of God. A specifically Christian understanding of God in turn arises from reflection on the story of Jesus. Christians do not think about God or the universe without thinking first about Jesus. In Jesus' humble, self-giving, suffering love we are given a glimpse of God's infinitely humble, self-giving and suffering love. These attributes are essential and not just accidental to God's being. Christian theology, therefore, must "read" evolution in the light of these three features.

First, evolution is an expression of God's humility. Even for creation to be possible at all, it is conceivable that God undergoes from all eternity a self-humbling, an emptying or pouring out—in Greek a *kenosis*. Reflecting on creation in the light of Jesus' kenotic love, expressed most vividly in chapter 2 of St. Paul's letter to the Philippians, some theologians have proposed that the omnipotent God humbly contracts or "withdraws" the divine presence in order to allow the world to be at all.

In light of the image of God who takes on "the form of a slave," creation may be seen as God's magnanimous "letting be" of something other than God. God must be "humble" in order to allow something other than God to emerge and become truly other. What evolution is really all about, then, is the world's being invited toward ever greater diversity, freedom and creativity in the presence of the humility of divine love.

Second, evolutionary creativity may also be read in terms of God's self-gift to the world. For theologian Karl Rahner the fundamental theme in Christian faith is that the infinite mystery of God pours itself out unreservedly into the creation. But since the Infinite cannot be received by a finite creation in any single instant, the world must undergo an ongoing self-transcendence, an expansion and intensification of its own being simply in order to receive this infinite gift. In its depth, therefore, evolution is *really* the world's adapting to the mystery of endless Love. This is why the world, including the human heart, is always restless. What is going on in evolution is the story of God's self-gift to the world and of the world's response to the infinite love that lets the world be itself.

Third, evolution is also a story of God's own struggle and suffering. If Christ is the incarnation of God, then the experience of the cross means that God takes suffering into the very center of the divine life. By virtue of creation's solidarity with Christ, we must assume, then, that the epochs of struggle and suffering in evolution—and not only human suffering—are also taken into God. What is going on in evolution, therefore, is the world's suffering along with the groaning Spirit of God toward new creation. Nature itself bears the shape of the cross. It also, therefore, bears the promise of resurrection.

43. Aren't the elements of chance, impersonal selection and vast amounts of time in nature enough to account for evolution, without invoking any notion of God?

Evolutionary materialists claim that the recipe for evolution is so simple that there is no room left over for theological explanation. In their view evolution requires only the three ingredients: chance, law, and time. By stirring up these three components, evolution blindly cooks up all of life's strange brew. Let me explain briefly:

First, evolution requires random, undirected occurrences. These include the accidental chemical combinations that brought about the first living cell capable of reproducing. They also include the chance genetic mutations that allow a few organisms to adapt to their environments so that they can survive and reproduce. And they include many other erratic events that shape the course of evolution (for instance, climatic changes or asteroid impacts that, by wiping out the dinosaurs, made room for mammals and eventually humans).

The second ingredient for making evolution is the deterministic "law" of natural selection that remorselessly weeds out the weaker organisms and allows only the strong to survive and reproduce.

The third constituent is time. Since evolution is such a hit or miss affair it requires enormous epochs of time in order to try out various random combinations. Most of these tries will be nonadaptive, so in order to have the few "hits" capable of surviving and reproducing, evolution needs a vast temporal amplitude. This is why it has taken life three and a half billion years to march from primitive cells to human beings on earth.

In an evolutionary materialist reading, the interplay of chance, impersonal natural selection and time can bring about living and even conscious beings all by itself. We don't need to read any deeper into the evolutionary narrative.

However, a theology of evolution is suspicious of scientific literalism as well as biblical literalism. It will try, therefore, to make the case that the raw ingredients of evolution flow forth from the depths of divine love, a depth that will show up only to those whose personal lives have already been grasped by a sense of God. By definition this deeper reading of evolution will be rejected by the literalist, whether scientific or biblical.

The very fact that nature can even lend itself to a literalist reading is a consequence of the humble, hidden and vulnerable way in which divine love works. The very possibility of giving an atheistic interpretation of evolution is that God's creative love humbly refuses to make itself available at the level of scientific comprehension. And it is because divine creativity does not show up (as "special creation") at this shallow level of reading nature that fundamentalists reject Darwin and many Darwinians reject the idea of God.

The only way beyond this literalism is to be open to the possibility that nature as well as the biblical text can be read at deeper levels.

44. What "deeper" meaning does a theology of evolution see in the features of randomness, lawfulness and abundant time that make evolution possible?

The three items that make up the evolutionary stew remain themselves completely unexplained, and indeed unexplainable, by evolutionary science. They are presupposed by evolutionary theory, but the theory itself does not explain why the universe is "set up" in the first place as such a fertile blending of contingent happenings, invariant laws and temporal duration. Discerning *in depth* why the universe is put together this way is the task of a theology of evolution.

Theology will understand the three evolutionary ingredients as grounded in the reality of a promising God—in other words, the God of biblical faith. The fact that nature has room for random (in the sense of undirected) occurrences opens the cosmos to surprising future outcomes. This is consistent with a God who relates to the world as a giver of promises for a new future. Randomness in nature makes room for novelty, for fresh life, and eventually for culture and the history of human freedom. The deterministic regularity of natural selection, and all the laws of nature for that matter, are also essential to a universe open to the future. For without a certain amount of predictability or consistency in nature everything would collapse again and again into utter confusion. No future would be possible. And, finally, the fact of time, essential to evolutionary experimentation, makes good sense theologically as the arena of God's promise for the world's future.

For theology, time itself is a gift, a gift of the always arriving Future that biblical faith associates with the mystery of God. Darwinian science requires generous expanses of time for evolution to make its long, meandering and momentous journey. Given enough time, evolutionists say, anything can come about, including human beings. But time must first be given, and a deep appreciation of evolution must inquire into the endlessly extravagant generosity that makes a cosmos of irreversible temporal duration and spatial magnitude possible at all.

Scientific literalism and religious fundamentalism, of course, will both read nature's openness to accident as "absurdity." They will characterize natural selection as impersonal and "blind." And they will view the vast evolutionary reach of time as prodigiously "wasteful." But the three ingredients of evolution make very good sense to a theology grounded in the revelatory image of God as humble, self-giving and promising love.

45. Don't theologians sometimes soften Darwin's "dangerous idea" so as to make it more theologically agreeable?

This happens quite often. Theologians don't always look closely at the dark side of evolution. However, respectable theology must not edit the findings of science in order to make the natural world seem more immediately digestible to our accustomed religious sensibilities. It is for this reason that I have avoided placing theology in dialogue with milder, non-Darwinian interpretations of evolution.

Along with most scientists I am certain that Darwinian evolutionists do not give us the whole story of nature, and that improvements will continue to be made. But as a theologian it is not my job to tell scientists what they should or should not be saying about nature. Theology, as Paul Tillich insisted, should never endorse a particular scientific theory for theological reasons.

Especially in the case of evolution, theology must deal with a clean and unedited version of the scientific information. In the long run, by facing any difficulties science poses, theology is not contaminated but enriched.

Unfortunately, religious thinkers sometimes tailor scientific ideas in a way that will make them seem more congenial to the religious mindset. But this is an extremely dangerous, even self-destructive, way for religious thought to carry on. It does not help the cause of religious truth if we trim the rough edges off the admittedly ragged evolutionary picture of life simply to make it more theologically digestible.

This, I believe, is what the defenders of so-called "Intelligent Design Theory" do when they discuss God and nature. (See questions 60 and following.) They are so intent upon proving that God is the direct explanation for all of the order in nature that they ignore the messiness implied in Darwin's picture of life. They think the best way to debate with evolutionists is to prove that the world is much more orderly than geology, biological science and paleontology actually demonstrate. However, such posturing not only fails to convert evolutionists to a religious outlook, it also fails to take advantage of ways in which the disorderly features of biological evolution may actually widen and deepen our understanding of God.

I don't want to give the impression here that the theory of natural selection gives us the final word about life, either. I think it is safe to say that Darwin's vision is only a small fragment of a much wider and still not fully manifested set of truths about the life-world. Like all science, Darwinian biology abstracts from the rich complexity of nature and cannot penetrate to its ultimate depths. My point is simply that theology must not present its own vision of truth in a way that fails to take into account the well-founded discoveries of biology, geology, paleontology, astronomy or any other science for that matter. Such a narrow perspective would only make the world seem too shallow for both scientific and genuinely religious exploration.

46. How does the figure of Christ fit into an evolving world?

St. Paul, St. John, and later St. Irenaeus and other Christian writers, developed what theologians call "cosmic Christology." In order to express the magnitude of God's redemptive love, these authors envisaged the presence and power of Christ as reverberating throughout the entire universe as it was understood in their respective times and cultures. Because of the Christ-event, they professed, we live in a whole different universe from that otherwise conceivable. According to St. Paul, for example, the crucified and risen Christ has crushed the demonic powers of the underworld, and will finally gather all the diversity of creation into unity under the dominion of God. And St. John saw the influence of the incarnate Word of God operative even "in the beginning," in the very creation of the universe.

This audacious extension of Christ's sanctifying presence throughout the universe has unfortunately been nearly forgotten. In modern times we have located Christ firmly enough within human history perhaps, or within our personal spiritual lives; and we have helpfully recovered the humanity of Jesus and his prophetic sense of social justice. But we have lost much of the early Christians' sense of the Redeemer's power radiating throughout the whole physical universe. Evolutionary science, however, provides the occasion for a renewed and expanded cosmic Christology.

In the twentieth century Teilhard de Chardin (1881–1955) and Karl Rahner, along with several other Christian thinkers, brought renewed focus to cosmic Christology. They emphasized that not only the evolution of life, but also the story of the entire universe has from the beginning been silently shaped by the Word of God who has appeared in the flesh during the evolutionary period known as human history, and who is yet to appear again in the fullness of cosmic time. Indeed evolutionary thought has provided the opportunity for an even richer cosmic Christology than that available to earlier Christian generations. It allows theology to picture our evolving universe, in all of its temporal and spatial grandeur, as moving toward an ultimate fulfillment, a new creation in the Christ who is yet to come.

Evolution, therefore, as Teilhard declares, is holy. And as the universe continues to grow in complexity and consciousness it becomes increasingly "Christified." To Christian faith Christology is inseparable from evolutionary cosmology. The whole story of the universe is simultaneously the story of Christ's gathering to himself a body—a body of which we and our creative contributions are a small portion. When we think of the Body of Christ, therefore, we must think not only of a human community, but of a whole evolving universe converging on Christ. And by partaking of the Eucharist we join ourselves not just to the human Christ but to the Christ whose body includes the entire evolving cosmos.

47. What will it mean theologically if we find that life has evolved elsewhere in the universe?

Is it conceivable that in all this vast universe our planet is the only place where life exists? Even before modern times, it is interesting to note, some religious believers took for granted that heavenly bodies, including the moon, were inhabited by living and intelligent beings. So far, however, there is not a shred of positive evidence that life, let alone intelligent life, exists anywhere else, although many scientists agree with Carl Sagan that the cosmos is probably "brimming over with life."

For centuries we humans thought that the earth was the center of the universe. Today our planetary position no longer seems so privileged. Modern astronomy has exposed the earth as an ordinary celestial body orbiting a rather average star two thirds of the distance from the center of a mediocre galaxy, the Milky Way. Astronomers have now identified the Milky Way as a spiral galaxy containing billions of stars (and probably many more planets) in an observable universe that contains more than two-hundred billion other galaxies.

Given all this immensity, and the rather "average" situation of our planet, the probability of life elsewhere would seem to be high. Indeed there is already evidence that complex organic molecules necessary for life do exist abundantly in outer space. And if Darwinian evolution takes place here, it seems quite likely that something like natural selection would be operative as a general law of nature.

Still, for life to exist on earth a great number of physical coincidences had to converge. So improbable are these many coincidences that today some scientists are reluctant to concede that life exists elsewhere. A few even suspect that our planet may be the only outpost of life in the entire universe. If that is so, in spite of the spatial mediocrity of the earth, if we grade things in terms of their physiological complexity, life here may, for all we know, be the pinnacle of cosmic evolution.

Nevertheless, a vital Christian faith should have no difficulty accommodating Sagan's universe "brimming over with life." If the incredible diversity of flora and fauna on this earth is any hint of the gracious extravagance of God, we should be ready for the discovery of a similar excess of divine creativity in other regions of the universe. The creative Spirit of God blows where it will, not only here, but also in provinces uninhabited by humans.

48. What if we find that beings more intelligent and ethical than ourselves have evolved elsewhere?

A scientific project called "The Search for Extraterrestrial Intelligence" (SETI) now hopes to find intelligent life elsewhere. Because of the almost unimaginable distances separating stars with potentially life-bearing planets, it is presently hard to imagine how we could easily communicate with so-called "aliens," even if they do exist. We might get scattered signals from them, and they from us; but since communication cannot travel faster than the speed of light, it would take as many as two-hundred thousand years just to get the reply to a message sent from one edge of our Milky Way galaxy to the other. This is considerably more than the amount of time we descendants of Cro-Magnons have been around.

Nevertheless, SETI is a project that Christian faith should have no difficulty supporting. It would be humbling, but entirely healthy, if someday we found out that we were not alone. Christian faith has not only survived but has thrived as a result of experiencing other blows to our human craving to be at the center of the universe. Were we to find that other intelligent beings, perhaps smarter and nicer than us, exist in the cosmos, this discovery should not disturb our own sense of self-worth.

Humans, it is true, have always had difficulty accepting alien beings, including ethnic groups within our own species and many other species of life on earth. Genuine Christian faith, however, encourages us to embrace, even to love, the "otherness" and diversity that evolution has brought about. If our technology eventually puts us in contact with exotic worlds and strange cultures beyond earth, the commandment to love our neighbors would be no less germane than before.

Even if extraterrestrial beings turned out to be more intelligent, more comely, more compassionate and ethically evolved than we are, Christian faith already has the resources to appropriate such a discovery. At the center of this faith is the image of a God of creative excess who, as Meister Eckhart wrote, loves all creatures with an infinite and impartial love. Conversion to Jesus' sense of the overwhelming generosity of God should already have prepared us to rejoice in the existence of beings that may in some respects surpass us.

Furthermore, as we grow increasingly aware of the fact that our arrogant domination of nature has led us to the brink of ecological catastrophe, it would be chastening to experience the noncentrality of humans in the total cosmic scheme. Ecologists almost unanimously agree that a major reason we treat the natural world so recklessly is our assumption that humans are the only or main reason for the creation of the universe. The discovery of extraterrestrial intelligence would be a helpful corrective to such an impression.

49. Is it appropriate for us to alter the course of evolution by genetic manipulation?

Science has made possible many technological advances that have alleviated human suffering. But it has also made way for appalling abuses. It would be naive to assume that technologies based on the new genetic knowledge will be immune to such tragic ambiguity. While scientific knowledge may be a good in itself, its uncircumspect application may eventually bring disasters that none of us can clearly presage. Those who are sensitive to the precariousness of life's past evolutionary achievements or to the delicate fragility of established ecosystems would urge that we avoid manipulating the genes even of plants and animals, not to mention humans.

The so-called "human genome project" has now completed a comprehensive decoding of our own genetic makeup. With each day researchers are finding out more about the complex ways in which segments of DNA provide information that shapes our bodily and mental features. Such meticulous deciphering of human life has never occurred before. It is hard not to be apprehensive about the eventual consequences of the new knowledge yielded by this bold undertaking. Above all, what are the religious and ethical implications?

To refrain from using our know-how to improve the quality of life would appear callous. But opinions will differ on just how the virtues of justice and compassion apply when it comes to genetic engineering. In the case of human genetic manipulation, the task of moral discernment is especially formidable. Can we responsibly intervene in or modify our genetic makeup? Would this be "playing God?"

Theologian Ted Peters, in his book *Playing God,* says not necessarily. Of course, humans are always prone to arrogance and abuse of their knowledge and skills. But, Peters points out, we are created in the image of a creative God. We have been gifted by God not only with the life we inherit from our evolutionary past, but also with a creative capacity and responsibility to carry life forward in ethical and ecologically wholesome new ways. We are, in the words of theologian Phil Hefner, created co-creators. God's will is that in this unfinished universe we participate in the work of making things new.

Many Christian ethicists now agree that "somatic" gene therapy, the objective of which is to heal individuals suffering from inherited diseases, is a humane application of the new knowledge. However, there is much more reserve when it comes to "germline" intervention which, if and when it becomes scientifically practicable, could conceivably alter the whole character of human existence. Today I think that most Christian ethicists would insist that, given our present ignorance of future consequences, drastic (germline) changes in the human genome would be irresponsible. In my own opinion, the potential for monstrosity looms so imposingly here that we should resolve as a species to refrain from such an abrupt intrusion into evolutionary creativity.

III.

CREATIONISM

50. What is creationism?

All theists accept the doctrine of creation, but the term "creationism" today usually refers to the beliefs of biblical literalists who reject evolutionary biology. There are several kinds of creationists. "Young earth" creationists hold that about 6,000 years ago God made the universe in six literal calendar days of the week as depicted in Genesis 1:1–2:3. God created Adam and Eve directly, and we are literally their descendants. Genesis is historically accurate, including the story of the "fall" of humanity and the curse on creation. Most creationists hold that the story of the flood helps to explain the catastrophes recorded in the fossil record. Accordingly, the theory of evolution must be false and even blasphemous.

"Old earth" creationists are more open to current scientific depictions of earth-history as being 4.5 billion years long. However, like other creationists they claim that the various kinds of life could not have been created by natural processes from inanimate stuff, but only by God's "special creation." Every species of life, as it is now classified by biology, was brought about by direct divine creation sometime in the remote past—and more or less in its present form. Distinct species could not have evolved from prior organisms. There might be incidental variations over time within a species, but new species cannot arise from older ones. This implies emphatically that the first human beings could not have evolved from nonhuman species of life. Human beings endowed with an eternal soul were created in their present form directly by God.

Creationists of all stripes generally take it that Adam and Eve were created perfectly in the garden of Eden and that a primordial sin by our first parents corrupted nature and humanity, thus requiring the redemption by a savior. If we humans had come about by way of evolution, this would mean that there was no primordial sin and therefore no need for the coming of Christ. Creation was whole and complete in the beginning, and whatever imperfections we now observe in nature, such as disease, aging, extinctions, suffering and death are the result of an original sin by Adam and Eve.

Needless to say, such an interpretation is hard to square with evolutionary accounts of life and the universe. The creationist reply is that science must be wrong whenever it fails to correspond with the plain meaning of scripture.

51. What is "scientific" creationism?

Scientific creationism accepts the tenets of creationism, but goes further, insisting that the biblical creation stories give us a more reliable *scientific* explanation of life than we can get from Darwinian biology. The proponents of scientific creationism, such as Henry Morris and Duane Gish, are usually trained scientists who profess to follow scientific method, though their assumptions about science are typically more Newtonian than contemporary. However, what is most surprising is that they take the Bible itself to be *scientifically* authoritative. They reason that if the Bible is literally inerrant, it cannot conceivably contradict science. Therefore, we should take the biblical stories of creation as scientifically factual. And since Darwin's views do not correspond with the word of God, we must conclude that evolution is false.

Scientific creationists go on to argue that since nobody has ever directly observed the evolution of one species into another, the theory of special creation by God is, at the very least, no less scientific than Darwin's ideas. Moreover, they are fond of saying that evolution is "only a theory" and not an established "fact." Gish admits that the accounts in Genesis have no scientific eyewitnesses, but he claims that this puts the Bible on at least an equal footing with Darwinian "stories" which are also unverifiable by immediate observation. According to the scientific creationists we have to choose between these two "theories," and the Darwinian one seems so utterly improbable and unbelievable that it only makes good sense to choose the biblical version.

Again, what is most interesting about this kind of creationism is that it takes the Bible to be a reliable source of *scientific* information. This is why its proponents feel justified in asking for "balanced" treatment of creationism alongside of Darwinism in high school classrooms in the United States. The assumption is that students should have the opportunity to make a choice here between two *scientific* theories, one better than the other.

Not only is such an assumption anachronistic and exegetically objectionable. It also trivializes the sacred texts by bringing them down into the same secular context as modern scientific discourse. It forces biblical texts into a competitive encounter with scientific treatises, and in doing so suppresses any religious meaning they might have.

No less noteworthy, however, is that some Darwinians—E. O. Wilson, Daniel Dennett and Will Provine, for example—reject the Bible because it doesn't deliver a quality grade of scientific information. They share with creationists the assumption that the Bible is subject to being evaluated purely in terms of scientific criteria. The difference is that scientific creationists see the Bible as a source of good science, while the evolutionary materialists see it as a source of bad science. In both cases we see instances of literalism—a failure to read either nature or the scriptures at deeper levels.

52. Shouldn't public schools be allowed to teach "creation science" as an alternative to Darwinian theory?

Many Americans, perhaps as many as forty percent, would say yes. Some do not object to discussing Darwinian theory in biology classes, provided that "fair" and equal treatment is accorded to the biblical creation accounts. Scientists rightly object, however, that such coverage is inappropriate because "creation science" is not really science at all. And the courts have generally agreed with scientists on this point. Still, some politicians publicly endorse creationism and are willing to tolerate creation science in the classroom rather than lose a significant percentage of their voters.

The theologian, however, would argue that to teach the doctrine of special creation in the context of a class in natural science is not merely a violation of scientific integrity, but even worse is an implicit abasement of religion. Situating sacred writings alongside contemporary evolutionary biology, placing them in a competitive relationship with science in the classroom, will only give students the impression that the Bible is essentially a compendium of information comparable to science. Teaching biblical creation accounts in the classroom implicitly desacralizes revered writings whose intention is to open us to holy mystery, not to enhance our store of scientific knowledge. Since science was not even remotely part of the biblical authors' culture, they could not

possibly have been trying to teach their readers scientific truths. Therefore, demanding that creation stories be taught to students as science is
not only irreligious, but anachronistic also.

Ironically, it is only because creationists already tacitly accept
modern science as the authoritative road to truth that they are so eager to
have biblical creation narratives taught in science classes. The biblical
authors themselves would be extremely puzzled at current efforts to
force their ideas into such a restrictive framework.

53. Is it possible to teach evolution in our schools without it sounding like atheistic propaganda?

Yes. But students have to learn that science deliberately and
rightly leaves out any reference to God when it tries to explain anything.
And, second, this exclusion must be understood as *methodological*
rather than *metaphysical.* Let me clarify this distinction.

By definition science leaves out, and must leave out, any reference to God. Science must try to explain things as thoroughly as it can in
purely natural terms. To fit God into an explanatory gap that science
itself may eventually bridge is to shrink the Creator into a "god-of-the-
gaps." If we locate God only in the dark regions of human inquiry, such
a deity will become obsolete as soon as science shines its lights in there.
We should instead seek to locate divine reality and religious understanding of evolution at an *ultimate* level of explanation, one to which scientific ingenuity can never penetrate in principle.

Science is methodologically naturalistic (or methodologically
nontheistic). It carefully excludes the idea of God from its attempts to
understand nature. Theology does not object to this deliberate narrowing
of the field of vision by science—as long as scientists don't take their
exclusion as a metaphysical one. The term "metaphysical" here refers to
what is real. A metaphysical exclusion would mean that God does not
exist at all and therefore can have no explanatory role, at any level, in a
hierarchy of explanations. As soon as a scientist claims that what science sees is *all there is,* the boundary has already been crossed from
methodological to metaphysical naturalism.

Some scientific books and instructors have a difficult time making
this distinction and keeping a steady hand on it. A teacher's or a textbook's
methodological exclusion of God can, without warning to the reader,

subtly turn into an ideological claim that divine influence is *altogether* superfluous to our understanding of life. A textbook or essay that presents itself on the surface as purely scientific can unexpectedly transform itself into what sounds like atheistic propaganda.

From a scientific point of view it is correct to say that natural selection is a creative factor in the evolution of life. But when a scientific book or textbook claims—or even implies—that natural selection is the *ultimate* explanation of life and its diversity, then this is no longer science, but belief. And so, if creationists are wrong to insist on bringing belief into the classroom, then so also are scientists who turn scientific method into the *ultimate* metaphysical explanation of life.

54. Don't scientific presentations of evolution deserve the creationist backlash?

Scientists and scientific textbooks sometimes present evolutionary science in such a way that it sounds almost like they are excluding *any* explanatory role for God in the creation of life. When religious people read these works they cannot help wondering whether this exclusion of God is simply a consequence of scientific method's concern for purity, or whether it is meant to be taken as a broad philosophical claim. Darwinian biologists sometimes give an ultimately creative role to "natural selection," which is generally understood to be blind, impersonal and unintelligent. This sounds as though the scientists are excluding God from having any creative role in life at all.

For example, in an earlier edition of the *Encyclopaedia Britannica,* the author writes that Darwin "showed that evolution was a fact contradicting scriptural legends of creation and that its cause, natural selection, was automatic *with no room for divine guidance or design*" (emphasis mine). And the noted biologist Francisco J. Ayala more recently has written that "it was Darwin's greatest accomplishment to show that the directive organization of living beings can be explained as the result of a natural process, natural selection, without any need to resort to a Creator or other external agent." And, he goes on to say, "Darwin's theory encountered opposition in religious circles...because his mechanism, natural selection, *excluded* God as accounting for the obvious design of organisms" (again my emphasis).

In reading such statements it is often difficult to tell whether the author's "exclusion" of God is meant to be taken simply as a methodological bracketing out of theological explanation—which is entirely appropriate in science—or instead to be taken as a defiant metaphysical claim that God plays no explanatory role at any level of the life process. Science, of course, must not appeal to the idea of God in its own explanations of any set of phenomena. Science is "methodologically naturalistic." And so, it is entirely appropriate for the biologist to "exclude" God when trying to account for evolution. Quite possibly this is what Ayala intends. But this legitimate methodological exclusion is often taken by religious readers to be a metaphysical exclusion as well. Scientists need to state clearly whether their exclusion of God is meant methodologically or metaphysically or both.

I have no doubt that many evolutionary biologists *do* view natural selection literally as the "ultimate" and exclusive explanation of life's design and diversity. In such instances sensitive religious readers can smell the aroma of materialism emanating from allegedly "scientific" tracts. If evolution is presented in such a way as to entail the view that matter alone is real, and that God plays no role at all—at any level—in the creation of life, can we be surprised that so many believers have difficulty with Darwinism?

What scientific authors sometimes fail to recognize is that there can be a rich hierarchy of explanations (see question 41 above). By this I mean that things can be understood and explained simultaneously at several distinct levels without one *excluding* the other. To claim that the explanation of life's designs by natural selection excludes theological explanation at any level is an expression not of science but of "scientism."

55. Aren't popular presentations of evolution also laced with philosophical assumptions that make it difficult for religious people to accept Darwinian science?

There is no question that some popular presentations of evolutionary science have an ideological overlay that is not properly part of the science of evolution. They go far beyond methodological naturalism into the murky realm of metaphysical naturalism and atheistic propaganda. As I mentioned earlier, the many well-received writings of

Richard Dawkins, for example, routinely present evolution to the public as though acceptance of the *science* of evolution requires an atheistic outlook. According to Dawkins, you cannot seriously embrace evolutionary science unless you first accept the premises of an inherently atheistic materialism.

"Materialism," let us recall, is the view that reality is ultimately pure "matter" and that there is no spiritual world, no God, no soul and no ultimate meaning to the universe.

Dawkins is not alone in identifying evolution as a materialist idea. Biologist Michael R. Rose, in a popular treatment, has recently written that evolution finds its most natural ally in materialism. Philosopher Daniel Dennett calls Darwin's theory a "dangerous idea" because it destroys any basis for belief in God or cosmic purpose. And Will Provine says that believing biologists must check their brains at the church house door. Evolution, he insists, logically entails philosophical materialism. I should note that Darwin, in his diaries, also occasionally flirted with materialism as the appropriate setting for his science, and this has given encouragement to many of his followers.

The paleontologist Stephen Jay Gould, our best known popularizer of evolution, has maintained that what makes Darwin so hard to swallow is not the science of evolution as such, but the "philosophical message" that comes along with it, namely, that life has no direction, that there is no purpose to the universe and that matter is "all there is." Apparently, as far as Gould is concerned, materialism is inseparable from Darwin's science. And if Darwin's science necessarily entails all this philosophical baggage, we cannot hope to reconcile science with theology, as Gould has lately been attempting to do.

This alloying of Darwinian ideas with metaphysical materialism, however, is not necessary at all. Gould's and others' evolutionary materialism is a confusion of science with belief, and as such it is no less questionable than scientific creationism's conflating Genesis with allegedly scientific information. In both cases there is an arbitrary mixing of science with assumptions extraneous to science. The fusion of science and belief (whether the belief be materialistic or biblicist) will surely prevent any genuine encounter of evolution and religious faith.

56. What response can I give to creationists when they insist that I cannot believe in God and evolution at the same time?

Only if you can offer a larger and more compassionate picture of God than the one creationists believe in can you hope to make any headway. Presenting yourself simply as a skeptic will usually drive creationists deeper into their certitude.

In my experience it is almost impossible to win an argument with creationists on how to interpret scripture. However, you may be able to show that you too approach the scriptures with great reverence, and that it is your respect for the deeper truths contained in biblical texts that leads you to reject literalism. Here you may communicate a sense that taking the Bible as a source of accurate science actually diminishes the sacred texts. Symbols and metaphors—and here you may appeal to theological tradition going back long before Darwin—lead us much deeper into the world of the spirit than literalism does. Taking the Bible's figurative language literally actually leads to a loss of religious depth. As theologian Paul Tillich would put it, we should take the biblical texts not literally, but seriously.

It is also important to have some familiarity with contemporary biology. Creationists are often quite skilled in reciting snippets of dubious information that *seems* to support their denunciation of evolutionary science. They are very selective in citing works, especially by maverick scientists, claiming that evolution has never been "proven." In particular they are fond of pointing to gaps in the fossil record that signal to them the absence of transitional forms. They interpret these gaps as "evidence" of special creation of each species by God. There are numerous scientific books today that explain these "gaps" quite well without resorting to the miraculous.

Finally, in your encounters with both creationists and evolutionary materialists (most of whom ironically also read the Bible at a literalist level) you will have to communicate a sense that there can be a hierarchy of truths and explanations (see question 41 above). This means, for instance, that the Bible may give us deep religious truths without having to be scientifically accurate. It is a blessing, in fact, that the scriptures were written in the "naive" narrative and poetic language of a nonscientific culture. If they had been composed according to the standards of modern science, most people of the past—who knew nothing of science—could never have gotten anything out of them.

57. If Darwin makes it impossible to take the biblical creation stories literally, what meaning can they possibly have for us?

After Darwin we are actually in a position to see deeper into the Bible's accounts of origins (which incidentally are not limited to Genesis) and their religious meaning than ever before. We no longer have to look to the Bible to satisfy our curiosity about "how things began." Science can do that better anyway. Instead we can now focus on levels of meaning in the creation accounts that hide themselves from us as long as we try to make them compete with the ideas of science.

In this age of science, in other words, we can actually see more clearly than before that the point of the biblical creation accounts is essentially religious. Genesis, for example, seeks to awaken in us a sense of gratitude for the sheer glory and extravagance of creation. It tells us, through two distinct accounts, that the universe is grounded in love and promise. It provides us with a reason to hope. It assures us, moreover, that our world is essentially good and that nature is not to be confused with God.

This last point deserves further comment. Today religious believers usually take for granted the idea that nature is good, but centuries ago not everybody did. It was tempting to attribute nature's nastiness to whimsical deities, or to see its capriciousness as the embodiment of demonic powers. In some instances ancient thought viewed matter itself as the source of all evil. It was not evident to everybody that nature is intrinsically good.

Today we know better than ever that nature can be erratic and even deadly, even while also being benign and nurturing. Cruelty exists in the natural world alongside of comfort and care. It is tempting, at times even today, to view nature as inherently evil or to attribute to the cosmos the attributes of impersonality. After contemplating Darwinian processes, some evolutionists have loudly proclaimed that nature is inherently malicious.

The staggering claim of *Genesis,* however, is that, even with all of its ambiguity, nature is essentially good. After Darwin it is hard for many people to believe this. However, we are enabled by evolutionary science to suspect that nature's ambiguity is consistent with the "unfinished" state of the universe. Nature, we must now realize, is still in the process of being created. Even in ambiguity there is promise, and this is the powerful message of Genesis.

To the extent that nature is not yet fully created it will inevitably harbor a dark side. But in the light of both the Bible and evolution we may read the natural world as pregnant with promise, allowing us daily to renew our hope for a final fulfillment in a new creation.

58. Can evolution be reconciled with the idea of original sin?

One of the reasons some Christians have had such difficulty with evolutionary biology is that it seems to contradict the idea that we inherit from Adam some kind of "original sin." In fact, though, it merely contradicts a skin-deep biblical literalism and not the substance of Christian teaching regarding sin and redemption. An awareness of the scientific notion of evolution may even help us arrive at a deeper and more meaningful understanding of original sin than we had before.

I've often heard fundamentalist preachers declare that if evolution is true, then there could have been no "fall" of humanity. And if there was no fall, then what need is there for a savior? Wasn't the whole meaning of Jesus' life and death to undo what Adam had done? But if Darwin is right, the argument goes, there could have been no actual Adam. So the coming of a savior would have been pointless. Consequently, in order to preserve the fundamentals of Christian teaching we should repudiate evolution. Here Darwin himself gets demonized as one more carrier of the sinfulness from which Christ must save us.

However, most theologians today would consider such an interpretation of sin and redemption extremely shallow. What exactly "original sin" means, moreover, has never been made perfectly clear in the first place. As understood by St. Augustine (A.D. 354–430) who coined the term *(peccatum originale),* original sin is a biologically-transmitted tendency to evil desires *(libido).* And it is especially because of the influence of Augustine that Christianity in the West has made so much of the notion. Other Christian thinkers, both before and after Augustine, have held less biological and less severe interpretations.

Original sin, according to contemporary theological interpretation, refers not to a specific act committed by a parental couple in the remote past, but to the general state of our present human estrangement from God, from each other and from the natural world as well. We are all born into a world that is already deeply flawed, in great measure by human greed and violence. We have indeed "inherited" environments, cultures and habits of being which mix bad with good. Thus the notion of "original" sin points to the fact that, simply by virtue of our being born into this ambiguous world, we are conditioned not only by what is life-affirming, but also by a whole history of evil and opposition to life.

The notion of original sin, in this sense, is important for constantly reminding us not only of our shared estrangement from our true Origin and Destiny, but also of our human incapacity to save ourselves from this state of affairs. It helps us realize that only God can rescue us, and that efforts toward self-salvation are futile. Thus the need for a savior is in no way diminished by our recent evolutionary knowledge. There is no contradiction between evolution and a realistic notion of original sin.

59. Is there a clear distinction between original sin and the selfish tendencies we have inherited from our prehuman evolutionary past?

Unquestionably contemporary biology does link our species to a prehuman evolutionary heritage in which a "selfish" struggle to survive was the dominant engine of change. Recently many biologists have attributed "selfishness" not only to individual organisms struggling to survive, but also to the genetic units of inheritance. Genes are said to be "selfish," in that they will do literally anything to get themselves passed on to the next generation, regardless of the cost in suffering to "higher" forms of life.

We humans are also said to be the unwitting carriers of "selfish" genes—microscopic despots that pull all sorts of ingenious tricks, such as making us have ethical and religious tendencies, just to get themselves into the next generation. If we were born without ethical and religious tendencies, the selfish-gene argument goes, we would kill each other off or give in to despair; life would cease and our genes would not survive. Interestingly, some evolutionists tell us that in the interest of scientific truth we must now abandon the very religious impulses that helped us survive and reproduce in the first place! The point is, many biologists now claim, the whole evolutionary saga seems to be built on selfishness of one sort or another, even when it makes us personally altruistic.

If this picture is true, then it might seem that St. Augustine's notion of original sin as something biologically inherited would not be too far off the mark after all. However, we have to be careful not to take some biologists' metaphors too literally. As Holmes Rolston has argued in his masterful book *Genes, Genesis and God,* the same evolutionary story that a cynic sees as run by gene-selfishness is, from another perspective, a story of *gene-sharing.* It is the sharing of genes across generations that allows for life's richness and diversity as well as community. Genes are not adequately characterized by the adjective "selfish."

In any case, the term "selfish," as applied to prehuman forms of life or to the properties of genetic units incapable of moral choice, is clearly inappropriate if we understand it in ethical terms. Furthermore, since as far as we know animals are not endowed with freedom of choice or with ethical aspirations, we should not judge their instinctual behavior according to our own standards of good conduct. Competition and struggle for survival among individuals and populations prior to the human were essential if life was ever to evolve from simple to complex forms.

Nonetheless, it appears that we do inherit instincts that run counter to our social, ethical and religious values. We have to keep these in check in order to live ethical or virtuous lives. But do we need to see them as a consequence of original sin? Certainly they mark us as ambiguous and unfinished beings. But I believe it wiser to understand original sin not in terms of the genetic continuity we have with the rest of life, but primarily in terms of the complex of social and cultural pressures that channel our native impulses in destructive directions.

IV.

Darwin and Design

60. Doesn't Darwin contradict our belief in an intelligent designer?

Darwin, along with many of his followers, concluded that the theory of evolution undermines the time-honored belief that the order or "design" in living organisms requires a divine designer. And so, if God is thought of primarily as an "intelligent designer," evolution does appear to challenge religious belief. However, if God is thought of not simply as the ultimate source of order (or design), but also as the source of novelty (as the biblical God "who makes all things new"), then evolution is consonant with biblical religion's faith in the God of new creation.

Before Darwin, many religious thinkers had argued that the lawful activity and orderly patterning in nature could not have come about by chance, but only by "intelligent design." And, of course, the intelligent designer had to be "God." Darwin, however, gave us a drastically different explanation of the design in living beings. He did not deny that nature is intricately ordered, but his theory implied that the complex patterning in living beings is the natural product of an enormously lengthy process of trial, error and adaptation. Thus there is no need to posit a divine designer to explain, for instance, why a particular kind of finch's beak is exquisitely adapted to crushing and eating the specific kinds of seeds in its habitat.

In order to account for such adaptive design in living beings all you need are random variations, the mechanism of natural selection, and an ample amount of time (millions and millions of years) to filter out the adaptive from the nonadaptive features in organisms. During the course of evolution most organisms have been too crudely "designed" to survive in their habitats, and so they died out, leaving no offspring. Only relatively few, the best adapted, were able to survive and reproduce. However, if we look closely even at the survivors we can see that none of them can be said to be "perfectly" designed either, including ourselves.

Evolutionary biology calls our attention to the ample evidence of imperfect adaptation, and to the colossally "wasteful" and clumsy history of experiments that lies buried beneath the even surface of extant life forms. Even a cursory look at the geological record raises disquieting questions for those who think we can find abundant evidence of "intelligent design" in nature. The present orderly facade of nature masks epochs of chaos, waste and suffering alongside of amazing creativity. The beauty of the present life-world has been purchased at an enormous cost. The benign view of a divine designer serenely in control of nature seems quite remote from Darwin's disturbing picture of life. The elements of chance, struggle for survival, blind selection of the strong and elimination of the weak suggest that nature can be ruthless and impersonal while also being astoundingly inventive. Can we blame religious people for getting upset about all of this?

If we are going to speak honestly and intelligently about God after Darwin we must do much better than simply polishing up old design arguments.

61. Shouldn't theology vigorously defend the idea of divine design against the Darwinian claims?

Today there is a small, vocal and well-funded coterie of Christian thinkers who claim that Darwinism has not destroyed the idea of intelligent design after all. Promoting what they call "Intelligent Design Theory," they are active on the internet and have published often in religious journals hostile to evolution. Recently they have gone to war against the prevailing evolutionary mind-set in the scientific world. They generally take the view that evolutionary science is a vehicle of materialist ideologues. Most scientists, however, consider this movement another wing of creationism.

In my opinion, Intelligent Design Theory is not quite identical with creationism, but it is still entirely too narrow and is a naive way of doing theology after Darwin. It is interesting that the obsession with design is very popular among conservative Christians today. Indeed journals such as *First Things* and *Christianity Today* regularly feature articles and editorial policies that come close to creationism in their denunciation of Darwin.

Theology's reaction to evolution, however, should not be one of desperately trying to defend the idea of intelligent design. Such an approach has only led religious thought to slice away grand portions of scientific data in order to salvage an excessively rigid and religiously narrow idea of God. This editing of the biological and geological record only makes religious thought appear dishonest in the eyes of good scientists. Much more preferable is a theological approach that embraces without flinching the "dangerous" new evolutionary story of life. What it will find is that Darwinian science, when purged of the materialist philosophical spin that some interpreters arbitrarily put on it, exposes us to a much more interesting—and religiously satisfying—understanding of God.

If evolutionists have made the designer-God problematic, they have not destroyed a deeper religious understanding of God as the ground of novel forms of order rather than of fixed "design." I would argue, in fact, that Darwin's ideas actually allow us to retrieve afresh the biblical notion of a God who "makes all things new" (Isa 43:19; Rev 21:5). Darwin certainly challenges narrow ideas of intelligent design, but this does not mean that his new science refutes the idea of God.

After all, why should we think of God principally as a "designer?" Isn't God also the source of novelty? And doesn't the introduction of novelty inevitably disrupt perfect design? Isn't God as much the source of instability as of stability? Shouldn't we think of God as One who disturbs the mediocrity of the status quo in order to bring about something new? If God is the ultimate source of order, God is no less primordially the source of novelty that sometimes has to disrupt order so as to overcome triviality and monotony. The God of evolution is the inexhaustible wellspring of *new* forms of order.

62. Doesn't God have at least something to do with the exquisite design in living beings?

Certainly. But in order to make this claim appropriately after Darwin we must first emphasize that God is also the source of order-disturbing novelty. And second, we must not locate our theological understanding of nature's design at the same level as evolutionary biology's own explanations in such a way that it competes with science.

At its own level of understanding—one that methodologically refuses to engage in any theological inquiry—science has a very good explanation of design. Take, for example, a fish's eye. It is round rather than elliptical, making it remarkably "adapted" to seeing under water. How are we to explain such a marvel? Before Darwin we would have spontaneously praised the Creator for "specially" making fishes' eyes so suitably fashioned for an underwater environment. It was easy to interpret such phenomena as evidence of divine "intelligent design."

However, evolutionary biology, like any other branch of science, is compelled to look for a purely natural explanation of design. At the level of scientific insight it is inappropriate to attribute design directly to any kind of divine "intelligence." For the evolutionary biologist, fish have round eyes because in the remote past swimming creatures with oval-shaped eyes could not see their predators, so they got eaten, losing out in the struggle for existence. They produced no offspring, while other marine animals, those accidentally endowed with rounder eyes, could see well enough to escape predators. These were the ones that survived and reproduced.

I think we should allow science to go as far as it possibly can in explaining adaptive design in such a "naturalistic" way. But I also believe that evolutionary biology is still only one level of a whole hierarchy of explanations needed to understand the story of life *in depth.* Theology can be part of such a hierarchy of explanations. Indeed I believe we must at some point appeal to theology to explain *in an ultimate way* why there is any order or design in nature at all—as well as why there is instability and process too. But it cheapens theology to bring in the notion of God at the self-restrictive level of scientific explanation. This, it seems to me, is what the intelligent design theorists do, and they deserve the criticism they receive from evolutionary biologists.

We can explain life and its complex designs on many levels without one level being opposed to the other. Physics for example can explain life's order and design quite adequately from a thermodynamic point of view without interfering with biological accounts. Chemistry too can explain life at its own level. And so can theology. Theology, as one level in a whole hierarchy of explanations, has a legitimate role to play in our accounting in depth for the fascinating design in life. Problems arise only when experts on one level claim that theirs is the *only and adequate* explanation of life.

63. Aren't you being too hard on the proponents of "intelligent design" theory?

The "intelligent design" advocates are rightly sensitive to the way some evolutionists conflate science with materialist metaphysics. But in attacking the evolutionary materialists they throw the baby out with the bath water. They discard good science along with the questionable philosophical assumptions of some prominent evolutionists. What is worse, they defend an idea of divine action that turns God into a tinkerer rather than a creator.

The intelligent design theorists introduce their theological notion of design in such a way as to place it in competition with scientific explanation. They don't allow scientists the freedom to explain design naturalistically, that is, without appealing to the idea of God. Why is this a problem? Because the only way science can ever explain anything is in a purely naturalistic (methodologically agnostic) way. Science must *never* appeal to the supernatural, or else it is no longer science. Yet the intelligent design proponents insert their designing deity at a level of explanation proper to science rather than theology. Their designer-God is a god-of-the-gaps. Because they think adaptive design and such phenomena as DNA are naturally improbable, they insist that science itself must appeal to supernatural explanation. However, such a leap takes them outside of science. They mistakenly treat the idea of intelligent design as a scientific idea.

What theology finds objectionable here is not the fact that at some point we must appeal to divine influence to understand our universe and the story of life in a deeper way than science. Eventually we must. The problem is *where* one introduces the idea of divine influence into an extended hierarchy of explanations.

Intelligent design advocates—themselves inhabitants of Flatland—are inclined to bring God in as a *part* of scientific explanation. Ironically they diminish our sense of divine creativity by making God a link (albeit the most important one) in the causal continuum in nature rather than the depth and ground of all natural causation. They introduce the idea of divine intelligent design in such a way as to discourage further scientific research. Scientists rightly take offense at this intrusion since there is always a lot more to be learned in a purely scientific way about design in nature. If we have to appeal to the notion of God every time we meet an impasse in scientific inquiry, what is the point of doing science at all?

64. Can you give an example of how "intelligent design" advocates inappropriately insert theology into scientific levels of explanation?

In a recent book entitled *Darwin's Black Box* the biochemist Michael Behe provides a good example. He points out that Darwin himself had confessed that if life's designs had come about by any other route than small, gradual changes, Darwin's theory would be proven wrong. According to Behe, however, the living cell includes mechanisms that are too complex to have come about step by step, as evolutionary biologists typically assume. These mechanisms, he says, are "irreducibly complex." This means that they cannot function at all, and so be selected by evolutionary process, unless all of their parts are simultaneously present and working harmoniously together. A mousetrap cannot catch mice unless its several parts are all working together at the same time. If you remove just one component the trap will not work. Similarly, cellular constituents like blood-clotting mechanisms can't function unless all of their complex and diverse components are present simultaneously. There can be no such thing as a gradual evolutionary construction of irreducible complexity. So Darwin, by his own logic, must be wrong.

What, then, is the real explanation of irreducible complexity? Behe concludes that it must be "intelligent design," since evolutionary science, by definition, can't explain irreducible complexity. Anti-evolutionist Christians have celebrated what they take here to be the defeat of Darwinism, and Behe (a Roman Catholic) now basks in the warmth of their approval. Meanwhile, scientists have responded by denying that the cell is irreducibly complex. Their opposition consists mainly of imaginative scenarios demonstrating how mousetraps and cellular mechanisms could have been assembled gradually after all, thus saving the Darwinian paradigm.

Whether the cell is irreducibly complex or not—and Behe's opponents may well be right in conjuring up plausible depictions of gradual evolution—the appeal to intelligent design here is a theological diversion, not a scientifically fruitful supposition. Moreover, even theologically speaking, the notion of God as a "designer" is too narrow and misleading.

Behe is right to appeal to theology, but not while doing science. And his opponents are correct in chastising him, but not always for the reasons they do so. Behe fails to recognize that ultimate explanations, whether of design or anything else, should never be brought in at scientific levels of inquiry. But meanwhile many of his opponents, at least implicitly, consider science itself to be the *ultimate* level of explanation. From a theological point of view they are still living in Flatland, and the irony is that intelligent design proponents decide to join them there.

Immersed in this dimensionless domain, materialist scientists attribute the ultimate explanation of life and evolution to the play of blind chance, natural selection and the immensities of cosmic time. Rightly recognizing that this explanation doesn't provide a fully adequate understanding of life, the intelligent design proponents anxiously, prematurely, and I believe inappropriately, introduce the notion of intelligent divine design into what is strictly speaking a scientific level of inquiry.

65. Is the Darwinian picture of life any more at home with the God of the Bible than with the notion of an "intelligent designer?"

It is not hard to sympathize with religious people who have found Darwin's critique of design unsettling, and who have then either ignored it or rejected it altogether. However, numerous religious thinkers, beginning in the last century, have found the Darwinian vision of nature quite compatible with an expansive faith in God. Some have even found, to their surprise perhaps, that Darwinian evolution provides a most appropriate framework for appreciating the God of biblical religion.

Evolutionary theory now forbids our thinking of God simply as a designer. But it does allow us to think of God in a more biblical way than before. It encourages us to recover the sense of God's self-effacing humility in allowing creation to have an experimental, self-creative quality that allows the world to be distinct from its Creator. It lets us think of God as the source of novelty—as "the One who makes all things new"—and not just as the source of some humanly idealized order. Even the countless imperfect adaptations in the Darwinian story of life, so scandalous to advocates of design, can lead us to sense more palpably that the universe is still being created.

Focusing on design freezes the world and overlooks the vitality that constantly cuts through the iciness of order. Evolutionary science, on the other hand, gives us a world still fluidly open to the future. It can therefore awaken in us the sense of a God who is always drawing the world from "up ahead," rather than pushing it mechanically from the past.

If God is pictured only as a designer, the world that this God "designs" would have no future. It would be a dead and finalized order, closed off to any new becoming. A world sealed shut to novelty would be utterly lifeless. A one-sided obsession with "intelligent design," therefore, suppresses the biblical trust in a God whose creative "word" is always a word of promise. A promising God is *still creating* the world, apparently through evolutionary means. Through evolution creation is opened up widely to indeterminate future outcomes. Intelligent design seekers are not looking to the future, but to a dead past. Darwin on the other hand impresses upon us the fact of an unfinished cosmos. This, in turn, allows us to recapture the theme of promise, the central theme in the Bible's vision of God.

66. Doesn't the improbable complexity of the living cell and DNA require miraculous interventions by a designing God?

Intelligent design advocates would immediately respond that special divine interventions are necessary here. However, to hypothesize miraculous interruptions of nature by God only digs a deeper hole for theology, while simultaneously placing it in a competitive relationship with science. For if God can so easily intervene in nature as to shape nucleic and amino acids into living complexity, then why doesn't God also intervene right now to put an end to life's suffering? And, if we can call upon special miracles of "design" whenever we can't explain life's complexity in a natural, scientific way, then why should we bother doing science at all?

There must be a better way to account for living complexity than either a pure naturalism that rejects the notion of God altogether, or a supernaturalism that must occasionally and arbitrarily appeal to the miraculous.

I propose the following. First, if I may borrow once again a rather Augustinian suggestion from scientist-theologian Howard Van Till, it seems reasonable to say that a creator has *richly endowed* the universe, from its opening moments, with the potential for evolving toward the kind of complexity we see in the cell and genetic DNA. Having done so, there is no need for God to fiddle with the cosmic process. The universe is given an internal capacity for *self-organization* that removes the need for special divine manipulation of physical channels of causation. If so, the emergence of life, cellular complexity and DNA can be understood as natural developments seamlessly interwoven with the entire universe. The sprouting of life and mind in the universe is analogous in some ways to the blossoming of an oak tree from the inauspicious beginnings of a simple acorn.

Second, I propose that God seeds the universe not with design but with the *promise* of a complexity that eventually becomes alive and conscious, at least here on earth, but quite possibly elsewhere in the universe also. The "word of God," which according to Genesis hovers over creation in the beginning, is a word of promise. The universe is inseparable from God's promise of a future. Indeed it seems necessary to say that the temporal and spatial unfolding of a self-organizing universe continuously moves through a "field of promise," consisting of all the possibilities offered to it by a gracious and generous God.

And third, I would suggest that in some sense God (or, if you will, the Spirit of God) *is* this field of promise. Ultimately it is the world's moving more fully into God, and God's quietly coming into the world in the mode of promise, that allows nature to evolve and self-organize in the direction of life and mind. Such intimate involvement with the world on God's part remains, however, completely outside of the range of scientific detection. Yet it can richly account, in an *ultimate* rather than scientifically precise way, for living complexity.

67. How can God create life without violating the laws of physics and chemistry?

From the point of view of physics, chemistry and other disciplines there is no violation of natural law when life comes onto the cosmic scene. Yet when the first living cell with nuclear DNA popped up, clearly something most extraordinary had happened in the history of the cosmos. A theology of evolution must find a way to express how God is intimately involved in the creation of life without this divine influence being taken as interrupting nature's consistency. Without threatening or intruding into science's own domain, how can theology envisage living complexity as the utterly free gift of God's creativity?

One way of understanding God's powerful but scientifically undetectable influence on the world is to think of how information works. As you read this page you are looking at blotches of black ink fixed onto a white page. If you didn't already know how to read, all you would see would be unintelligible black marks. You would miss the informational content embedded here. Likewise, the presence of information is undetectable to physical science. Any ideas inscribed on this page, for example, will go unnoticed by chemistry as such.

And yet clearly information is present if we move to a deeper level of understanding. It steals onto the page very quietly and unobtrusively, in a manner hidden from the science of chemistry. It does not interrupt or strain the chemical laws that allow ink to bond with paper. It goes unobserved if all you're looking for are these laws and their effects. If you did not know how to read, and someone asked you to explain the page before you, all you could say is that a printing press had stamped black ink on a white page chemically suited to soaking it up. The informational content would not even enter your mind.

Analogously, biochemistry and evolutionary biology are, at least as such, incapable of detecting any deeper "informational" dimension that might be coming into the universe from an ultimate source of meaning. New possibilities, such as the emergence of living and conscious beings, can be actualized in evolution without their informational content ever showing up at the level of chemical or physical analysis. And the actualizing of these possibilities no more requires the violation of scientific laws than the inscribing of information on the page before you violates the chemistry of ink and paper.

So when the double-helix structure of DNA emerges in evolution, the informational aspect of life settles into the world in a way that does not interrupt or violate the laws of chemistry and physics. It seems plausible to hypothesize that God's relationship to nature, including the creation of life, is analogous to the quiet but effective way in which information enters into any medium. This, however, is only an analogy.

68. Can't you be more precise about how God interacts with the world in its evolution?

No. Precise language would diminish our appreciation of God's creativity. Trying to be too clear about something so fundamental as how God is involved in the creation and evolution of life will only make theology seem superficial.

I believe that much of the apparent conflict between science and religion, and especially between evolution and the idea of God, stems from our longing to locate divine action at a specific point in the realm of determinable secondary causes. Scientific skeptics, disappointed that they can't find any such causal intersection, summarily dismiss the idea of God as superfluous to evolution. Meanwhile creationists and intelligent design advocates claim that divine creativity is present after all—at the same level of inquiry that skeptics fail to see any such thing at all.

By insisting that God brought about new species by interventionist acts of "special creation" divine action is reduced to banal manipulation. The compulsion to fit God into a series of (scientifically available) causes in nature is rooted more in a desire to control than to worship. For the God of religion is always by necessity a hidden God, and God's unavailability to scientific experiment is essential if God is to be the ultimate ground of all causes. To insist that the *ultimate* ground of nature squeeze itself into a scientifically determinable series of efficient or mechanical causes is to eliminate arbitrarily any place for divine creativity in nature at all.

Nevertheless, it is appropriate to think about God's radical and continuous creation of the world in metaphorical ways. Metaphors are absolutely essential whenever we speak of things that are too big for us to clarify. Even science uses fuzzy metaphorical language to explain the complexities of evolution since the mathematical discourse of microphysics is too specific to grasp the historical drama of nature. Evolutionists resort to terms like "selection," "struggle," "adaptation," "blindness," "accident," and so forth, since too fine-grained a language would not be helpful for something so sweeping as the story of life.

All the more then is it appropriate for theology—which supposedly takes the widest possible view of nature—to think metaphorically of God as the "depth" and "ground" of life and its evolution rather than as a specific link in a causal chain. Further, in the biblical context it is also appropriate to think of God as the world's Future. In the Bible God is a God of promise. By opening up a future for the world, God creates and sustains it continuously without becoming a part of the world. It is the coming of this Future that makes the world evolve in the first place. As the world's Absolute Future (Karl Rahner's designation), God is the ultimate explanation of evolution. This is the God Teilhard de Chardin had in mind when he referred to the cosmos as resting on "the future as its sole support," that is, upon a God who is "less Alpha than Omega." This is the God of Abraham, of Moses and Jesus, the God of new creation.

V.

DIVINE PROVIDENCE
AND NATURAL SELECTION

69. Doesn't Darwin destroy the idea of divine providence?

Darwin's picture of life may at first give you this impression, at least until you dig deeper. Most of the variations—we now call them mutations—that evolution requires as "raw material" for bringing about new forms of life are nonadaptive, so they quickly die out. Only by accident do a few variations turn out to be "fit," in the sense of having a good chance of surviving and reproducing. Those countless organisms unfortunate enough to be burdened with nonadaptive traits are dismissed into perpetual oblivion by the remorseless impersonality of natural selection. Here we see on exhibit a universe in which randomness is compounded by what most of us would consider an excessive amount of wastefulness and cruelty.

Can we reconcile such a world with religious trust in divine providence? Natural selection's callous disregard of weaker organisms makes us wonder whether the God of this universe really "cares" for the most vulnerable living beings. Darwin seems to have destroyed the basis for belief in a providential God. To some scientific thinkers evolution is "rife with happenstance, contingency, incredible waste, death, pain and horror." Any God who creates and oversees such a world must be, therefore, "careless, indifferent, almost diabolical," and not "the sort of God to whom anyone would be inclined to pray" (David Hull).

Can religious trust in a providential God, then, survive Darwin? Not long ago a former Christian clergyman sent me the following reflections, indicating why he was now an atheist: "How could a loving God have planned a cruel system in which sensitive living creatures must either eat other sensitive living creatures or be eaten themselves, thereby causing untold suffering among these creatures? Would a benevolent God have created animals to devour others when he could have designed them all as vegetarians? What kind of deity would have designed the beaks which rip sensitive flesh? What God would intend every leaf, blade of grass, and drop of water to be a battle ground in which living organisms pursue, capture, kill, and eat one another? What God would

99

design creatures to prey upon one another and, at the same time, instill into such creatures a capacity for intense pain and suffering?"

Much of the religious world reacts to this portrait of nature by simply declaring that evolution must be false. However, as in the case of many previous challenges to our religious trust, I believe that we should face the evolutionary picture of things head-on. We should neither reject nor refashion reliable scientific information to fit our inevitably narrow concepts of deity. Of course, evolutionary biology is not perfect and will keep undergoing revision. But too much time and energy is wasted trying to show that evolution is wrong, when religious believers should be asking whether our understanding of God might not be too small to accommodate Darwin's world.

Providence means that the world is cared for by a loving and powerful God. But we must not be too simplistic in trying to understand how divine care manifests itself. In my opinion, evolutionary science invites us to deepen our understanding and appreciation of the doctrine of providence.

70. Has theology succeeded in reconciling divine providence with evolutionary biology?

Not to everyone's satisfaction.

Some interpreters, as we have seen above, keep looking for evidence of divine providence in instances of "design" in living beings. However, Darwinian (and neo-Darwinian) biologists tell us that most of what we consider "design" in organisms is the consequence of millions of years of blind trial and error experimentation. It is hard for many of them to see the hand of God in this process. Richard Dawkins declares that the cruelty of evolutionary selection is just what we should expect if, at bottom, the universe is pitilessly indifferent.

In response, some religious thinkers have lately begun to locate the providence of God in the cosmic constants and conditions that had to have been "set" with great precision at the time of the Big Bang if the universe was ever to give rise to life in the course of its unfolding. Taking their eyes momentarily off of the troubling story of life, they look for evidence of divine design in the physics of the early universe.

Others think they can see a general directionality in evolution that hints at divine guidance. For example, they point to the overall rise in organized complexity and corresponding intensification of consciousness over the course of evolutionary time. Perhaps providence is quietly guiding the cosmos toward some unimaginable culmination.

Still others see the providential hand of God directly implicated in the very severity of Darwinian process itself. God, they surmise, has set up here on earth a "soul-school," and the cruelty of Darwinian process is an essential part of its pedagogy. Without encountering difficult challenges, according to this view, terrestrial life and human souls would not be challenged to go beyond themselves. They would succumb to stagnation. In this interpretation the severity of evolution is the direct consequence of God's providential concern, not an obstacle to our trusting in it. Here there is no need to edit evolutionary science in order to make it compatible with a "schoolmaster" idea of God.

However, we should note that the idea of a God who directly "designs" a world so full of cruelty is no less repugnant to many sensitive religious believers than to evolutionists like Dawkins. Moreover, this pedagogical interpretation, while it does not have to trim off repugnant features of evolution in the way that design arguments usually do, is still too anthropocentric. It does not give a good answer to the question of why billions of years of struggle by innocent nonhuman life was necessary before our alleged "soul-school" came about. Hopefully there are better approaches.

71. How, then, would you propose that theology think of divine providence after Darwin?

I would prefer to reflect on evolution by starting with the understanding of divine providential care as this is given to us in the rich experience of our religious traditions. For me this means that rather than thinking of God primarily as a designer or a schoolmaster, I must begin with the sense of God as humble, self-giving, promising love. This is the image of God that Christians see embodied in the person of Jesus of Nazareth. In fact, Christians are advised not to think about God at all without thinking of this man and his character as depicted in the gospels.

Theology should ask what kind of world we should expect if divine providence takes the form of humble, self-giving, suffering love (see question 42 above). If this is what divine providence consists of, then shouldn't we expect to be living in a world very much like the one evolutionary science has given us?

Scientific skeptics, of course, interpret the prominent role of chance in evolution as evidence of a universe unguided by any providence whatsoever. They consider evolution's severe requirement that countless individuals and species lose out in the struggle for existence to be a refutation of the notion of God's watchful care. But theological reflection on evolution in the shadow of the cross can conclude that all of the available scientific evidence for evolution is quite consistent with a God who cares for the world enough to allow it in some way to create itself. Evolutionary data are completely consonant with the image of a God who is humble enough to allow something truly other than God to emerge spontaneously. Evolutionary science in no way contradicts belief in a God whose compassionate providential concern is that the world not be dissolved into God, but that it emerge as sufficiently autonomous to form a partnership with God.

Evolution's randomness, for example, seems consistent with a God who loves freedom enough to let the world be and become itself, that is, something distinct from its creator. The "blind" regularity and consistency of the "law" of natural selection is one of many "habits" the universe has had to develop in order to have any internal coherence at all. And the prodigious amount of time evolution requires is what we should expect if God is providentially concerned that the world be given ample opportunity to become itself. Providence is not a simplistic guarantee of safety. Rather it is the ground of opportunity. But opportunity is not devoid of risk.

Finally, the self-emptying God of religious faith does not stand aloof from evolution, but enters into it, taking all of its suffering and creativity into the divine life. Certainly this God is one who providentially cares for the world.

72. Theologically, what can we make of all the mutants, monstrosities and other accidents in evolution?

Our awareness of evolution requires an explanation not only of order, but also of the nonorderly, random and maladaptive aspects of the process. Are these also part of a providential scheme?

Modern science allows us to realize that the universe is still being created. Never before have we been so aware of the fact that we live in an unfinished universe as we are now. Our theology, our thoughts about God, must reflect our new understanding of nature in process. If we still wish to think of God as providential, therefore, we must now confess that God is not only the origin of cosmic order, but also the source of the evolutionary novelty that constantly stirs up, and often temporarily confuses, present orderly arrangements in nature.

Reflecting on evolution, theology may at least vaguely ascertain some meaning in the bizarre, random, undirected occurrences that otherwise seem so absurd to our limited human (including religious) perspectives. Strange and unpredictable events in natural history are characteristics that we should anticipate in a universe that is still unfinished and open to new creation. Without such deviant events the cosmos would long ago have become so rigidly locked into a fixed order that it would have remained lifeless and mindless. Order alone is not enough to give us an interesting universe. The cosmos also need events that move it beyond any presently-given state.

Present instances of order must give way if the cosmos is to let in new forms of order. We designate as "accidents" those events that do not fit into our present sense of order. Such irregular events, including strange and mutant forms of life, are not antithetical to a broad notion of providence. Our demand for a perfectly ordered universe is implicitly a demand that providence take the form of dictatorship. But God apparently has other ideas about what providence means.

God cannot be anything other than love. And love, as process theologians have often emphasized, inevitably respects the freedom and spontaneity of the world. This means that there must be room in God's creation for random events. And some of these events will perhaps seem peculiar, especially to our narrow human tastes. It is instructive, in this connection, to read God's humbling words to Job: "Where were you when I laid the earth's foundations?" (Job 38: 4).

We should not expect that evolution will be smooth and steady, following a course that corresponds to our own sense of appropriate direction. What a withered and leaden world that would be. Our ideally ordered world would be devoid of the craziness caused by accidents, but it would be a monotonous world. Evolution suggests that divine providence sees much further than we do. In this sense, once again, Darwin helps us to enlarge our sense of God.

73. How can we reconcile the *impersonality* of blind natural selection with the existence of divine providence?

Though evolutionary materialists consider the impersonality of natural selection to be evidence that the universe is utterly godless, religious faith requires that we take a longer and wider view of things. There is no question that natural selection works blindly and indiscriminately. But, then, so does gravity or any other "law" of nature. Without the predictable invariance of its rigid laws, nature would collapse into utter caprice and chaos. In principle, therefore, the remorselessly consistent character of natural selection should raise no more serious theological problems than do the laws of physics.

If you are still troubled by natural selection, however, try to imagine what life would be like today if evolution in the past had favored weak organisms rather than strong ones. If this had been the way things worked, life would have listlessly ebbed from our planet long ago. Certainly you and I would not be here.

Whenever questions about the wisdom of natural selection arise, it is useful for us to ask what the alternatives would be. What kind of universe would we have created? Would we have made one in which there were no challenges whatsoever to living beings? If so, would life have ever evolved to more complex and eventually conscious modes of being? And doesn't life have to confront and surmount challenging obstacles even in order to be alive at all?

Without encountering both the support and the constraint of physical law, could matter have ever transcended itself so as to become alive? And, having become alive, could it ever have become so complex, rich and diverse as it has if it had not come up against the rules of selection? Further, if everything were so accommodating that organisms never had to struggle at all, would life ever have become conscious and self-aware? And would religious awareness ever have been awakened without conscious life having experienced the realities of fate and death that raise for conscious beings the question of life's meaning?

The remorseless regularity of the "law" of natural selection, moreover, is simply one more expression of every finite entity's need for boundaries in order to be actual at all. In a sense, everything that exists outside of God must be limited in order to be anything definite. This limitation is itself providential. Without borders it would be hard to identify anything as concretely existing. I would suggest, then, that the fact of selection is ultimately no more an obstacle to religious faith than any other law of nature. Gravity too, after all, can be cruel if we happen to be falling from a dangerous height.

74. Many biologists claim that natural selection is creative enough all by itself to eliminate any need for a creative and providential God. Isn't this the case?

Darwin allowed room for the existence of a remote First Cause of the universe. But at best this was the do-nothing God of deism, a God who supposedly created the world "in the beginning" but did not care to become involved in its day-to-day workings. By removing God from intimate involvement with the world Darwin appeared to make natural selection the only and adequate creative agent in the sphere of life. Natural selection, given enough time, could apparently account for all the various kinds of living organisms all by itself. God is apparently not a factor.

There is no question that natural selection is creative. The question for theology, however, is whether it is creative in a way that makes God superfluous or in some way diminishes the role of God as creative and providential. Does Darwin make it more difficult or less difficult for us to believe that God is "Creator of all things visible and invisible" and that God numbers the hairs of our head?

Today many of Darwin's followers think that natural selection renders obsolete the idea of such a God. But usually they are talking about the God of "special creation." Evolution does force theology to steer away from the idea that God makes ad hoc creative interruptions or repairs in nature. If God is the Creator of life, it must be in a more intimate and fundamental manner than this. Are we to imagine that the Creator enters into the world of nucleotides (the "letters" in the genetic code), splicing them together into DNA segments, inserting them into the cell to create the first living being, and then goes away only to return when a new species needs to be created? If so, why are there so many deleterious mutations?

Shouldn't we instead learn to think of God's creativity and providence as more global, intimate and foundational to the entire universe than the role of occasional tinkerer allows? By locating God's creativity and providence at a more comprehensive level of explanation we can avoid the notion of a puttering deity. And by abandoning the adventitious idea of special creation we also allow science to go on in complete freedom in its own characteristic efforts to clarify the process of life's origin and evolution.

There is, at least in principle, no danger that scientific clarification will ever do away with our sense of the mystery that underlies the existence of life. But let us not locate "mystery" at places where there are still humanly solvable "problems." To do so is both intellectual and religious suicide.

75. How can I respond to those who insist that natural selection contradicts divine providence?

To say that natural selection leaves no room at all for divine providence is not a scientific but a philosophical claim. It is a kind of *belief,* one that simply assumes (without proof) that we cannot find a deeper way of understanding life than that of biological science.

So common is this claim among contemporary biologists that many religious people feel obliged to react to it with equally strong claims that all living species were brought about not by evolution but by God's *special creation.* What both sides fail to grasp is the possibility that evolution and divine providence can both be fully and simultaneously involved in the ongoing creation of life.

Traditionally theology has associated God with a level of explanation known as *primary causality*, and nature with *secondary causality.* As primary cause God is the ground of being, the ultimate explanation of the whole context in which ordinary events—occurrences in the realm of secondary causation such as natural selection—take place. As the world's primary cause, God is responsible for the world's existence and continuation; this God does not abandon the world after creating it but remains intimately present to it, sustaining it and underlying all that happens in the world.

This God is in no way the remote and uncaring absolute of deism. Put otherwise, God is the ultimate but unspecifiable "power of being" underlying all scientifically specifiable creative processes. For theologian Paul Tillich divine providence is not a magical rescue operation. Providence means that there is no situation or occasion in which the world, life and human beings are cut off from the sustaining divine ground of being.

If scientists complain that divine providence is not evident or observable in evolution, you might simply point to the power present so abundantly in evolutionary creativity. Or you may even point to the power present in your own protests against the cruelty of nature and the apparent silence of God. The reality of providence wells up within us whenever we experience the courage to go on with our lives in the face of suffering. Providence is the ultimate font of the power of self-affirmation manifested in all living beings and in the general cosmic conditions that make life possible. This is a God closer to us than we are to ourselves.

76. But don't you have to agree that the idea of natural selection fits more comfortably into a materialist than into a providential view of the world?

The biologist Richard Dawkins, and his philosophical supporter Daniel Dennett, certainly believe so. Dennett, as we have seen above, calls Darwin's notion of natural selection a "dangerous idea," meaning that any of us who believe that God influences nature had better not look too closely at evolutionary theory if we want our faith to survive. Evolution, he argues, is a completely impersonal process. Nature unfolds according to simple rules in the same way that a computer program does. Evolution, in other words, is an "algorithmic" process. Through blind selection of adaptive changes, over a period of three and a half billion years, evolution, according to Dennett, has blindly and aimlessly produced all the diversity of life, including human intelligence. No providential deity plays any role in the process.

Dawkins argues that the fundamental units of biological evolution are the coded segments of DNA known as "genes." Gene-survival is the driving force in evolution. It is the nature of genes, he says, to maximize opportunities for their survival and reproduction. Blind physical necessity drives genes to do whatever they can to secure their immortality. Natural selection impersonally weeds out all the reproductively unfit sets of genes in each generation of life. This blindly selective process is sufficient to explain all the products of evolution, including us. What need, then, for divine providence?

In response I would say that any judgment that evolution is an inherently materialistic or atheistic notion is not itself a strictly scientific claim, but instead a belief *about* science. It is rooted in the belief system known as "scientism." This belief rapidly spawns the correlative ideology known as "scientific materialism." And these two beliefs are not products of scientific inquiry, but *gratuitous assumptions* that arise from social and individual preferences that have nothing inherently to do with science, including biology.

Theology is especially sensitive to those places where Darwinian scientists cross over the line from science to materialist dogma. Although theology must not object to purely scientific ideas, even when they seem to be very challenging, it *is* permitted to debate issues of ideology or belief that sometimes get mixed up with science.

In answer to your question, then, a theologian may legitimately deny that evolution is any more at home in a materialist setting than in a providential one. Theology cannot prove this. But it can still plausibly contend that the novelty, vitality and creativity of evolution make very good sense if we see them as manifestations—ultimately—of the "power of being" that theology refers to as providence.

77. What reply can I give specifically to the atheistic evolutionary claims of Richard Dawkins and Daniel Dennett?

You might begin by simply pointing out that it is not science itself but a materialist interpretation of science that underlies their atheistic evolutionism. It is helpful to remind them that it is never permissible to mix science with a particular belief system, whether it be materialism or biblical religion. Although one cannot do science without having some background beliefs about reality, these beliefs should not become part of science itself. When Dawkins and Dennett (along with others like Stephen Jay Gould and E. O. Wilson) insist that evolution is a purely materialist, purposeless process they are already imposing a specific ideology upon the scientific data. By conflating materialism with evolution they are in no position to criticize creationists who mix science up with ancient biblical texts.

Of course, it is impossible to avoid interpreting scientific information in terms of one or another set of *background* assumptions about what is "really real." These assumptions make up what is called "metaphysics."

All of us have metaphysical assumptions, and it is important to become aware of what they are. For the religious believer there is an implicit theological metaphysics that claims that God is the *ultimately real,* whereas for the materialist, impersonal matter (and its equivalent energy) is, at bottom, all there is.

Both of these metaphysical positions lead to assumptions about the scientific data that science as such has no business talking about. The materialist believer may say that Darwin provides a firm foundation for scientific skepticism, but this is not a *scientific* conclusion. And the religious believer will say that "evolution is holy" since it is rooted in a promising God who is already incarnate in matter. But this too is not science, but metaphysics.

Those who embrace the notion of divine providence will rarely get very far in conversation with materialist evolutionists by simply bringing in more scientific data, although it is certainly relevant to do so. And the same is true when scientists dialogue with creationists or "intelligent design" devotees. Different background assumptions will cause people to frame scientific information in very different ways. What is at issue in these encounters is not science, but beliefs or metaphysical commitments.

Perhaps, then, the best you will be able to do is to argue that the evolutionary data is "consonant" with a theological metaphysics. You will not be able to prove your religious viewpoint by appealing to data that is inevitably ambiguous. What you can do, however, is argue that nature's ambiguity, including its dark and tragic features, is consistent with our living in an unfinished universe. And an unfinished universe, one that is still being created, may not be devoid of promise. Moreover, a theological metaphysics has the advantage of being able to give a good rational explanation for why there is a universe at all rather than just nothing. At some point, as Hans Jonas argues, we need to account for the "naked existence" of the world. For him and many others among us, it is impossible to avoid theology, at least at this point.

78. Is there any direction or purpose to evolution?

It depends on what you mean by "direction." If you mean "heading straight toward a goal fixed from all eternity," then evolution seems directionless. All the random experimentation and wild meandering, along with the apparent "wastefulness" of the process, certainly makes us wonder whether we are witnessing the unfolding of a divine plan. Paleontologist Stephen Jay Gould, for example, has repeatedly stated that the Darwinian vision necessarily implies that life and the universe are directionless. When scientifically uneducated believers hear or read such stark claims, perhaps it is not hard to understand why they want nothing to do with evolution.

However, we can still plausibly contend that the universe *as a whole* has advanced in a *general* direction since the time of cosmic origins. At the very least the universe for billions of years has been in the business of bringing about living and thinking beings. In an even broader sense there has been an ongoing cosmic trend toward complexity, and toward more and more intense versions of ordered novelty—that is, toward *beauty*. At the beginning the universe was a monotonous sea of radiation. Now there are plants, animals, persons, cultures and religions. Let us not minimize the fact that great complexity and beauty have emerged in this universe.

In my experience very few Darwinian biologists bother to look at the larger story of *cosmic* evolution. Many of them simply assume that the vast realm of cosmic matter is inherently indifferent or even hostile to the emergence of life and mind. And since the material universe seems essentially hostile or indifferent to life, the best explanation for life and all of its ramifications is a combination of aimless chance and blind necessity.

Perhaps, though, we should train our vision less narrowly on biological processes and instead look at the whole universe more carefully. Let us take in the entire cosmic process within which Darwinian evolution is a relatively recent phase, at least here on earth. What do we see when we stretch our vision across fifteen billion years of cosmic evolution since the big bang, remembering that life here has been around only during the last four billion or so? Is there no directionality to this grand cosmic epic?

Since the moment of cosmic origins, by anybody's standards, we know that there has been a gradual rise in organized complexity, in sentience, and eventually in conscious awareness. After all, we *are* here, so at least something of importance has happened. The universe's evolution has lately produced minds. The existence of your own intelligent personhood should be enough to make you suspect that something of *importance* has been going on in the universe, for you cannot help valuing your own mind. Even if you are questioning or doubting what I have just said, it is because you implicitly value your own intelligence. Can a universe that produced your (inevitably valued) mind be *essentially* pointless? If you think so you have just contradicted yourself.

If we understand purpose as the "orientation of a process toward the realization of a value," then it is hard, without logical contradiction, to deny that the universe—at least in the minimal sense just sketched—has a direction or purpose. To say that the invention of mind is the only purpose of evolution, however, would be extremely narrow-minded.

79. Why does evolution have to be drawn out over such a *prolonged* amount of time?

Evolution implies that the universe was not completed in a single moment in the beginning. We now know that we live in an unfinished universe. So why didn't God finish creating at the time of origins? Why all this "fooling around" for *so much* time?

In 1873, not long after Darwin presented his ideas, the Russian theologian Vladimir Solovyev (1851–1900) asked the same question. He was part of the first generation of religious thinkers to become familiar with Darwin's ideas, and it is instructive to look at his own response. "The full answer to this question," he wrote "is contained in one word, which expresses something without which neither God nor nature can be conceived; the word is *freedom*."

I don't know whether we can improve much on this response. It must be because God wants the world to be something other than God that the Creator allows evolution to take place in the messy, meandering, drawn-out manner that it does. Divine providence, in other words, wills the independence of creation, not just at the human level but throughout natural history. Maybe this is why the world and life have unfolded only gradually. And who are we to decide how long this should take?

A nonevolving world, we may safely conjecture, would be one that had been created complete and perfect in the beginning. But an originally perfected universe would not possess the future indefiniteness in which alone freedom can take root. If things had been completed in the beginning, the world would have been rounded off and finalized in such a way that there could be no future opportunity for freedom ever to become actual. For freedom to exist there must be an indefinite realm of yet unrealized possibilities up ahead, in the future. A world that lacked the open horizon of yet-to-come surprises would quench the sparks of freedom from the very start. In creating a world for freedom God created time, a deep unfathomable immensity of time.

Nobody, of course, can claim to comprehend the works and ways of God, but I believe theology can at least make good sense of the fact that the world was not brought to a state of finished perfection in the beginning. A nonevolving, nonbecoming world is theologically inconceivable, as Teilhard de Chardin has emphasized. Any theology in touch with the value of freedom should already have anticipated that the world would be something like the way Darwin has pictured it. Try to imagine a world without the possibility of chance occurrences, or one devoid of an enormous temporal magnitude in which to unfold. I think most of us, upon careful reflection at least, would not prefer a temporally stingy world in which ample scope for the actualizing of freedom would have been snuffed out from the start—even if that meant a world devoid of tragedy.

80. Does evolution imply, then, that God has no fixed plan for the universe?

In order to embrace the doctrine of divine providence it does not seem necessary for us to imagine that God has an inflexibly deterministic "plan" or design for the universe, if by this we mean that every event has been allotted its specific place from the beginning. Any prefabricated divine blueprint, specifying just exactly where everything will fall out, would be incompatible with God's grace. It would not fit in with God's concern for the world's future and God's gift of freedom. It would be hard to maintain that God loves such a world fully.

God's "plan," if we still prefer to use the term, cannot mean a predetermination. Perhaps, then, we should speak of God's "vision" for the cosmic future. In more biblical terms we might speak of God's *promise* for creation, rather than of a fixed plan for what the world may become. A plan or design, as the great French philosopher Henri Bergson insisted, would close off the future and render our own lives essentially pointless, since all outcomes would already have been laid out in advance. And in Teilhard de Chardin's words, if we truly believed that everything is already decided, it would surely "clip the wings of hope."

Biblical faith entails a world in which hope and promise can flour-ish. It is a great gift to faith and theology that Darwinian evolution pro-vides us with just such a world. In an evolutionary context a sense of promise, and trust in God's promises, can emerge and thrive. Nature, if I may say so, is not a perfected plan but a promise of perfection. When we read in Genesis, and again in the Prologue to John's Gospel, about the "Word" that hovered over creation "in the beginning," we may under-stand this "Word" not as a blueprint, but as God's promise or vision of what the world might become.

Evolution, therefore, does not have to follow a fixed arrangement. And for that very reason the world is infinitely deeper, more open, more dramatic, and more interesting than any world imagined to be com-pletely passive or submissive to a rigid divine scheme. The God of evo-lution does not determine all outcomes in advance but allows the world to have a part in shaping its own future.

Viewed theologically, therefore, it is not surprising that evolution takes so much time, for by definition a finite world can never drink up the sea of the Infinite. A finite world can never fully adapt to its inexhaustible Origin and Goal. The great gulf between the finite and the infinite sum-mons forth a great drama of evolution across endless eons of time.

81. Why would God want to create a world that becomes increas-ingly independent as it evolves?

Whatever God does, we may safely assume, is done out of boundless love. But love always wills the freedom of the beloved. Divine love longs, therefore, that the whole creation be, and increasingly become, "other."

To dramatize this point, perhaps we should ask ourselves once again how we would have gone about creating the world. Would we per-haps have made a perfect world, one devoid of "wasteful" expanses of time and removed from any possibility of suffering and death? Would we, if we had the power, fashion a completely finished product, one that corresponded in every respect to our own will?

Such a cosmos would not be truly distinct from us. It would be nothing more than an extension of our own being. We could not deeply love such a universe since it would not be really other than us. Love, to repeat, requires an "other." So a creator who refused to risk allowing the world some degree of independence could not truly love it. It is the very nature of divine goodness to generate otherness. And it is because God is infinite generosity that God wills the independence of the world.

So the universe will never be forced into a straitjacket devised from all eternity. Instead the universe will possess a strain of indeterminacy, a potential for emergent freedom. Even from the time of its most primitive physical origins the universe showed promise of independence. Physicists today find a kind of "indeterminacy" already present in the mysterious subatomic layers of the universe. Evolutionary biologists point to another strain of indeterminacy in the "random" undirected genetic mutations and other contingencies that make the emergence of new species and the general diversity of life possible. And we humans discover an even more momentous installment of the world's emerging independence in our own capacity for free choice. All of this has become clearer since the time that science has discovered evolution.

I cannot emphasize enough, therefore, what a gift evolution can be to our theology. For us to turn our backs on it, as so many Christians continue to do, is to lose a great opportunity to deepen our understanding of the wisdom and self-effacing love of God.

82. Isn't this "God of evolution" a powerless God and not the mighty God of the Bible?

In Christian faith, as St. Paul testified so passionately, God's power (by which I mean God's capacity to influence the world) is paradoxically made manifest in the vulnerable defenselessness of a crucified man. But as theologian Edward Schillebeeckx has rightly observed, God's vulnerable defenselessness is not equivalent to weakness. Vulnerability, he claims, can "effectively disarm evil" much more powerfully than can brute force. So this is by no means a powerless God that we are talking about here. This is a God who can bring about much grander effects than could a deity conceived of in the crude manner of dictatorial power. This is a God powerful enough to create a world endowed with freedom and self-creativity.

When Christian theology talks about the question of providence and evolution it must do so in terms of a specifically Christian understanding of God—not of some aloof, abstract "intelligent designer." In Jesus' defenselessness on the cross, we are gifted with an image of God that seems perfectly congruent with the evolutionary character of life.

The randomness, the struggle, and the seemingly aimless meandering disclosed by evolutionary science may be incompatible with a divine designer, but they are not incompatible with a power that takes the form of defenseless love.

If God were "powerful" only in the vulgar sense of having the capacity to overwhelm or annihilate, then the facts of evolution might be theologically troubling. But a divine power that manifests itself in infinite love does not seek to manipulate or dissolve that which it loves. By seeking intimacy with a universe distinct from the divine being, God longs to preserve the difference and otherness of the cosmos. It is in God's capacity to form an intimately dialogical relationship with the world that God's power comes to expression. Such power invites evolution to occur.

Not surprisingly, a God whose power is intent on allowing genuine *otherness* to emerge concedes to the world its own autonomous principles of operation. In this concession there is no deficiency of truly authoritative divine power, for it is a power that lets the other be. Our own petty experience of the crudity and willfulness of dictatorial power in human affairs provides a poor analogy for understanding the divine capacity to summon an emergent, extravagantly diverse, universe into being.

How effective, after all, is coercive power, even in the human sphere? At best it can manipulate things or persons only externally. It can never influence beings from within, but only superficially from without. In the presence of a vulnerable, defenseless love, however, the world is allowed to experience its own internal power—a power of self-creativity that eventually takes the form of human freedom. God's power is manifested most fully in God's self-emptying empowerment of the creation.

83. Can the vulnerable God of Christian faith be reconciled with the notion of God's power to create a universe from nothing?

It is easy to lose sight of the immeasurably good news implied in the doctrine of creation. Only a little reflection shows that a Creator who could bring this vast and complex universe into being from nothing could also lead our own lives to the fulfillment for which we long. Faith that the world is not self-originating, that it is grounded in a Power beyond itself, means that in spite of all the absurdities of the present we may still hope for *new* creation.

But have we thought often enough about just what *kind* of divine power could give birth to such a universe? If God is the originating Reality, how can there be a world that is truly other than God? What must happen to God in order for anything distinct from God to come into being?

It is a great paradox that God creates the universe, yet allows it to be in some sense independent. How can we reconcile our idea of divine creative power with a universe that exists "on its own" and that eventually produces life and humans who possess a freedom even capable of opposing God?

These are old questions, but recent science has put a fresh slant on them. Scientific studies of evolution and of the phenomena of "chaos" and "complexity" show that our cosmos, unfolding over a period of about fifteen billion years, is very much a self-creating reality. I don't mean to suggest that nature is the only source of its own existence, but the universe now appears to be anything but the passive product of a determining divine force. As scientists today agree, the world is composed of *self-organizing* systems. The sequential arrangement of physical stuff into atoms, molecules, planetary systems, stars, galaxies and clusters of galaxies, cells, organisms, persons, societies—all of this takes place in a way that seems to require no outside manipulation. Even the emergence of the universe at the moment of the big bang now appears to physics to have happened "spontaneously."

Let us add to this puzzling picture of a self-organizing universe the consensus of evolutionary biologists that the creation of life, including humans, has not been accomplished through one instantaneous act of divine magicianship. Rather, the story of life's taking shape on earth has involved countless experiments in the self-ordering of adaptive systems. In view of this widely accepted picture of nature forming itself, how can we still think of creation as also the *ex nihilo* product of divine omnipotence?

Some scientists bluntly reply that modern science has now rendered the notion of creation by God completely superfluous. However, the new scientific picture of a spontaneously self-organizing universe actually provides Christian faith with the opportunity to renew and deepen its unique understanding of divine power. It allows us to see more clearly that divine creativity is inseparable from the self-renunciation of divine love. The greatest exercise of divine "power" is that which humbly allows something other than God to emerge into being. The divine power to create *ex nihilo* is paradoxically rooted in the divine humility.

84. How can God's creative power arise from the "divine humility," and how can this help us make sense of evolutionary phenomena?

Christian faith, because of its Trinitarian vision of God, cannot separate God's identity or God's work in creation from the event of Jesus' crucifixion. The very essence of God as self-giving love is revealed to us in Jesus' death. In some way, therefore, Christian theology must learn to think about God's creation and the whole story of the universe in the context of the cross.

Referring both to his glorification and his death by crucifixion, the Johannine Jesus proclaims: "If I be lifted up I will draw all things to myself." This image suggests that the most glorious form of power is that which humbly invites other beings to enter into organic unity with God of their own accord, and not out of compulsion. The aura of freedom in which the early Christian community emerged into being around its "lifted up" and newly-risen Center may provide us with the key to how God's power works in all of creation.

The cross reveals a God who creates the universe not so much by manifesting coercive might as by humbly "withdrawing" (to use our imperfect language) so as to allow the entire universe to emerge into being "spontaneously" and uncoerced. God's power to create is not a crude act of force but an event of "letting-be." As the theologian Jürgen Moltmann puts it, "Even in order to create heaven and earth, God emptied himself of all his all-plenishing omnipotence, and as Creator took upon himself the form of a servant."

In the mysterious "nothingness" opened up by God's creative selflessness the universe is invited to emerge *ex nihilo* and to swell forth into continually new being under the guidance of God's poured-out and now indwelling Spirit. Thus the self-organization of nature—including its evolutionary meandering—seems contradictory only so long as we forget that God's power is most mightily expressed in humility. Once we learn to think of God in the light of the reality of the crucified Christ, the spontaneity evident in nature and the freedom we feel within ourselves are compatible with belief in a powerful Creator.

85. Does this humble "God of evolution" who seeks the "otherness" of the world have any support in theological tradition?

I believe we can find support for this understanding of God not only in the New Testament but also in the church's Christological traditions. What emerges from the early disputes and councils of the church is a resolve, sometimes molded in the face of powerful opposition, that the humanity of Christ must not get dissolved into the divinity of Christ. Christ is fully human not in spite of but because of his "hypostatic" union with God. In the relationship of Christ's divinity to his humanity we are given a glimpse of how God relates to the entire world.

Christ's human nature, according to the Council of Chalcedon (A.D. 451), must not get lost in the divinity to which it is united. God clearly wants to relate to a world that is "other" than God. In Christ's human nature, Christians believe, the whole universe somehow subsists. So in the Christian way of looking at things, God's presence to the world does not dissolve the world into God any more than the divine nature nullifies the humanity of Christ. The dominant intuition here is of a God whose power and effectiveness is expressed in the longing for the self-coherence and autonomy of that which is other than God.

The temptation to fuse Christ's human nature into the divine, thus denying the real humanity of Jesus, is known as monophysitism (from the Greek roots meaning "one nature"). Monophysitism is a recurrent temptation of Christian faith, and it is still around. Indeed much religion, and some kinds of "mysticism," long for a monophysitic kind of annihilation of the world in God. However, I believe the characteristic Christian instinct is to foster the sense of an eternally differentiated union of the world and God. To seek an undifferentiated, homogeneous oneness of ourselves or the world with God is an expression of monophysitism.

Underlying the uncurbed craving for a "designer" is a persistent, but questionable, longing for the kind of divine presence or power that refuses to permit the world any real independence. To avoid the risk and uncertainty of evolution, the intelligent design proponents seek a universe immediately and rigidly crafted by God, instead of the much more substantial and interesting one that must blossom indeterminately over a long period of time from its interior resources. They seek safety in an abstract cosmic order rather than rejoicing in the liberating novelty and emergent freedom that give such rich meaning—but also the possibility of tragedy—to the story of the universe and life.

The God of evolution, however, is not a "presence" that obliterates the particularity and uncertainty of creation. Rather, this God invites the world to become more and more independent so that God's dialogical relationship to it will be all the more exquisite.

86. Isn't a God who seeks the world's independence the God of deism all over again: a God, that is, who is not intimately involved with the world?

Not at all. In fact, what I am calling the God of evolution is paradoxically much more deeply involved with the world than any deity who interfered and constantly tinkered with creation. The God of freedom loves the world enough to endow it with the creative potential to unfold from within itself without needing magical interruptions. God's care for creation is expressed more sublimely in allowing the creation to have a degree of autonomy—with all the risks this involves—than in forcing the world to take a particular course. This is a much deeper kind of "providence" than that implicit in design arguments.

Giving the world space and time to become itself does not mean that God is not near to the world or deeply intimate with it. The divine Spirit is poured out into the world and is interior to the process of creation. We may even say that God's creative Spirit is the ultimate explanation of evolution. The world is embraced constantly by God's presence. But this presence does not show up as an object to be grasped by ordinary awareness or scientific method. It is not empirically available, in other words. Nor does it coercively manipulate things. Its influence is unobtrusive and immeasurable. Only those attuned to religious experience will be aware or appreciative of it.

This presence of God to creation consists in part of God's offering the world fresh new possibilities for becoming. As the world moves into the future it can become different from its past. Science has shown clearly that this has been the case for fifteen billion years. Why, we have every right to ask, doesn't the world stay stuck in a particular pattern? Why such cosmic restlessness as science has disclosed? Why do the universe and life continue to change?

The world is restless to evolve only because there exists a realm of possibilities yet to be actualized. But these possibilities, as the philosopher Alfred North Whitehead has emphasized, do not just float in from nowhere. They must reside somewhere. Where do they come from? Whitehead's answer is "God." In a manner deeper than science can ever detect, God graciously grants the world new possibilities for evolving. As the world makes its way from matter to life and consciousness, and then to culture and religion, new possibilities are always made available to it. The ultimate source and repository of these possibilities is "God."

It would be most inappropriate to conclude, therefore, that this generous divine stimulus to evolution is in any sense uninvolved with the world. Though the world may "wander around" experimenting with all the rich possibilities available, this leeway is consistent with a God who does not force the world to take a particular direction. Without in any way stifling the independence of creation, God remains humbly present to it—with an intimacy that is unimaginable.

VI.

EVOLUTION, SUFFERING AND REDEMPTION

87. What sense can theology make of all the suffering in evolution?

Sooner or later all theological reflection comes back to the question of theodicy: how can we justify belief in a God who permits suffering and evil? Evolutionary science adds nothing qualitatively new to this tormenting question. If theology has never answered it satisfactorily in the past, we can scarcely expect it to do so now.

For many scientific thinkers, however, the science of evolution has clearly aggravated objections that have always been leveled against the idea of God, including those we find in the Book of Job. Why does God allow all the suffering and waste in the millions of years of evolution? Scientists speculate, for example, that over ninety-nine percent of the species evolution has produced are now extinct. What sense can we make of the epochs of suffering and loss that lie beneath the surface of nature's present order?

Any response theology might give to the question of suffering will inevitably fall short. However, according to Christian faith, the passion and resurrection of Jesus present us with the portrait of a God who shares fully in the suffering of this world and who rises victoriously over it. There is no easy theoretical solution to the problem of suffering, but we may hope for an eschatological one: God will "wipe every tear from their eyes, and there shall be no more death or mourning, wailing or pain…" (Rev 21:4). We can assume that this final consolation applies to the whole of the life story and not just to the human episodes.

The struggle and pain in evolution are certainly not contrary to a Christian interpretation of the world in terms of the cross of Christ. Christian experience, moreover, implies that suffering can have a transformative quality. If we are attuned by faith to the conviction that suffering can lead to something higher, then we will not be completely taken aback by the Darwinian picture of natural history. And if we frame the whole of nature within the scheme of hope and promise of resurrection, Christian faith allows evolutionary process to be redemptive as well.

The stumbling block to accepting Darwin, then, is at root the same as the real challenge of Christian faith, namely, that we embrace the cross as part of a journey leading to new life. For if through faith one can accept the scandal of the cross, then one can be prepared for the kind of world depicted by Darwin's science. The evolutionary picture challenges simplistic versions of natural theology, but it does not contradict the central religious teaching that suffering, in spite of being intrinsically evil and something we should resist with all our might, can be given a higher meaning. Struggle, says Holmes Rolston, III, is the dark side of creation. "The question is not whether the world is a happy place, but whether it is a place of significant suffering through to something higher."

88. Does God actually "suffer" along with the evolving creation?

Darwin's revolutionary new ideas seem to require that we bring our sense of God closer to the whole of creation than we may have done earlier in modern times. Evolutionary thought helps us move beyond the aloof apathetic deity of so much pre-Darwinian piety. I believe, along with many other theologians today, that only the notion of God as self-emptying love makes sense after Darwin. This is the God who suffers along with creation and saves the world by taking all of its evolutionary travail and triumph into the everlasting divine compassion. This is not a God that theology invented just to accommodate Darwin. This is the empathetic God revealed in the pages of the Bible. This is the God of Israel who felt the pain of the oppressed in Egypt. It is the God who identifies with the Crucified. This is the God that Christian faith encountered long before we learned the story of nature's evolutionary birth pangs.

The theme of God's vulnerable self-giving love has always been implicit in Christian faith. The doctrine of the Trinity implies that Christ's life, suffering and dying are internal to, not outside of, God. Yet, as the philosopher Alfred North Whitehead has rightly noted, when we formally fashioned our images of God in the West, the image of Caesar often won out over that of the humble shepherd of Nazareth. Unfortunately, the image of God as "dictator" still lives on in our religious sensibilities—and in much theological protest against evolution—even though faith in the incarnation has in principle thrown it out.

Today, though, partly as a result of our awareness of the long tortuous trail of suffering depicted by Darwin's story of life, the idea of a God who is sensitively exposed to nature's distress is beginning to emerge more explicitly. By turning our attention to the previously hidden chapters in the great drama of creation, Darwin's ideas stir us to bring our thoughts about God into deeper accord with nature's long struggle, including that of our own species.

Sensing the living presence of Christ in their midst, the early Christian communities were able to discover a surprising new meaning in the suffering and crucifixion of Jesus. Jesus' pain and death, they reasoned, must be redemptive. Suffering, therefore, need not be seen as punishment—since Jesus was innocent—but instead as a gift for others. And if suffering can become grace, this can only be because the suffering of Jesus is in some mysterious way God's own suffering. Because of Jesus' incarnational solidarity with all of nature and history, the suffering in these realms is assimilated into the life of God where it takes on an unfathomable but redemptive meaning.

89. Can the God who suffers along with evolution also be powerfully redemptive?

At the heart of Christian faith lies the image of a compassionate (literally "suffering with"), self-emptying God. Theologically we may argue that this self-humbling is not just a posture that God assumes for a brief time during an "earthly" incarnation in the historical life of Christ. Rather it is an attribute that exists in God from all eternity. We should not think of God as ever having existed in any other way than as humble, self-giving, empowering, promising, redemptive love.

Theologians differ on the question of whether "self-limiting" is essential to God's nature or an activity undertaken "freely" by a God who could also have chosen not to be creative. We may assume that ultimately God's freedom is inseparable from divine love, and since love needs an "other" in order to be actualized, the world's existence is the expression of a free—in the sense of unrestrained—love. The need for another is not something that limits love, but allows it to be actualized. There is no a priori necessity, however, that any *particular* universe be the one that exists. Others are also contingently possible.

At any rate, theologian Jürgen Moltmann speculates that it is the eternal "self-humbling" of God that makes creation and redemption (new creation) possible in the first place. From all eternity God's creative love is grounded in a divine self-emptying. In this sense God never changes. Whenever we think about the universe and its evolution from the perspective of Christian faith we might keep before us this image of an eternally self-humbling God who allows a world to come into existence in relative independence, and who simultaneously pours forth an infinitely redemptive love into it.

As long as we fail to take seriously this disturbing image of God's humility, the existence of God will quite likely appear incompatible with a Darwinian world. But if we make central the picture of a self-giving God who renounces any impulse to shape the world independently of the world's participation in the process, then the discovery that life unfolds the way evolutionary science pictures it should not take us completely by surprise.

The suffering of living beings, therefore, is not undergone in isolation from God, but becomes part of God's own story. In the context of infinite compassion—as faith encourages us to trust—the world's suffering and tears will be washed away and redemption made final.

Any attempt to make philosophical sense of God's paradoxically redemptive power-in-humility is doomed to fail. However, if in faith we allow our lives and hearts to be transformed by the image of a vulnerable God, we may be able to view evolutionary suffering and struggle in a uniquely redemptive way. By seeing it all as God's own suffering, we can hope for an ultimate victory of love and life over pain and death, even if we cannot understand why suffering is so abundant in the first place.

90. Doesn't Christian faith, therefore, already anticipate something like the Darwinian picture of life?

Yes. In a way, we should not have been so surprised at the Darwinian picture, or more recently at the scientific news that the whole universe is evolving.

What *is* truly surprising—and perhaps too hard for any of us to accept fully—is that God's creative power would become manifest in such an unbelievably self-effacing fashion. The idea of an almighty God who remains untouched by the world's suffering is hard to reconcile with Christology, but for some reason we keep hankering for a God modeled on Caesar rather than on the figure of Jesus. The Christian picture of God is so revolutionary that every age seems to have trouble digesting it. In my opinion, one of the advantages of our coming to grips religiously with "Darwin's dangerous idea" is that it now literally compels us to dig down more deeply into the root system of Christian faith.

John Macquarrie has noted that the picture of divine humility at the foundations of Christianity has contradicted everything people had believed about the gods. The God of Jesus is utterly unlike the Marduks and Jupiters, as well as all our traditional images of God understood as a divine potentate or "designer." Theology is offended by evolution only when it assumes a rather imperious concept of divine omnipotence. Such a bias, of course, only leads us to expect that the world will be a perfectly ordered paradise. So when we find out about the clumsy and experimental character of evolution we easily grow disillusioned with the almighty Orderer. Darwin himself moved toward agnosticism as a result of his inability to reconcile the randomness, struggle and impersonality of evolution with the benign, regimenting deity of much nineteenth century "intelligent design" theism.

Evolutionary science, however, demands that we give up once and for all the tyrannical images we may have sometimes projected onto God. The real stumbling block to reconciling faith and evolution, therefore, is not the sufferings in nature and human history, but our failure to have acquainted ourselves sufficiently with the startling image of a God who seeks the world's freedom and who shares fully in the world's pain.

91. What does our hope for "redemption" really mean in the context of evolution?

Redemption after Darwin is best understood as St. Paul understood it: as *new creation*. Our hope is for the renewal and fulfillment of the whole cosmos, not just the salvation of our individual souls.

If God is truly love, then this love would invite and persuade, not compel, the cosmos to reach beyond itself toward new modes of being, towards new creation. We should not expect a world graced by divine love to be frozen immediately into finished perfection. Such a "finished" world would be lifeless and devoid of any genuine future. If God is love then we should be surprised if there were not a good deal of movement and indeterminacy in the world, including the random mutations that provide the material for evolution's prodigal experimentation. In evolution, with all of its ambiguity, faith may be able to discern at least dimly the coming of new creation.

In such a universe, of course, there is room for ambiguity and evil, including suffering. The evolutionary portrait of nature suggests that God somehow wants the world to "become itself." As the divine Love gives itself to creation, the world's independence and freedom do not decrease but intensify. And when humans emerge in this most fascinating story, evolution becomes endowed with an unprecedented freedom and consciousness. But this freedom brings with it a capacity for sin. Faith in God, however, entails faith in redemption. Evil, suffering and sin can be conquered by new creation.

At its most basic level, evolutionary thought opens up the future in a manner unknown to our religious ancestors. Once we realize that we live in an unfinished universe, the cosmic future becomes full of possibilities for surprising outcomes that we had never dreamt of before. A new kind of trust and hope can blossom in this open-ended universe if only we allow it to do so. The future can be fresh and very surprising. It may even bring new meaning to a world which at present seems hopelessly lost and even absurd. Hope for redemption can become one with our new sense of a world still being created.

92. But isn't the evolutionary future uncertain? Why should we trust that there will be any meaningful outcome to the process?

There is no denying the uncertainty of the future, and despair is always an option for us. But without our taking a chance on hope for new creation we may be going against the grain of life and evolution itself.

As many great religious thinkers have taught, what most effectively conquers evil is not the stoical practice of virtue, but trust in the future and the ultimate worthwhileness of our lives within this universe. In terms of our present awareness of cosmology and evolution this means that only a passionate conviction that the *whole* cosmic journey is leading somewhere important will adequately energize our ethical lives to work toward the good.

Recently Vaclav Havel, president of the Czech Republic, expressed a similar sentiment. "I have become increasingly convinced," he said, "that the crisis of the much-needed global responsibility is in principle due to the fact that we have lost the certainty that the Universe…has a definite meaning and follows a definite purpose." As long as we believe the world is a pointless process it is hard to imagine what might nurture ethical commitment consistently from one generation to the next. But how do we know that the cosmic journey leads somewhere? The answer is that we don't. Ambiguity does not go away. We can only trust. And perhaps the fact that we must always fall back on trust rather than clear vision is itself due to the fact that we live in a still unfinished universe. In a finished or perfected world there would be no shadows and no doubt. That we walk by faith and not by sight is a condition that accompanies our status as part of a world still in the process of being created. But in a universe still coming to birth perhaps only faith and trust can allow evolution to move forward into a new future.

We must be resigned to the fact that by trusting we are making a wager, taking a risk. But our faith and trust may very well be the way in which the universe continues to evolve creatively. Perhaps we might not relish the notion that the world's future balances so delicately on our capacity for trust. But, as Teilhard de Chardin puts it, the only way forward is through a "great hope held in common." In his book *Activation of Energy* he goes on to claim that it is only the trust underlying our religions that can carry forward the world's evolution: "What is most vitally necessary to the thinking earth is a faith—and a great faith—and ever more faith. To know that we are not prisoners. To know that there is a way out, that there is air, and light, and love, somewhere, beyond the reach of all death. To know this, to know that it is neither an illusion nor a fairy tale. That, if we are not to perish smothered in the very stuff of our being, is what we must at all costs secure. And it is there that we find what I may well be so bold as to call the *evolutionary role* of religions."

VII.

TEILHARD DE CHARDIN
AND ALFRED NORTH WHITEHEAD

93. Who is Teilhard de Chardin?

It is impossible to talk seriously about the question of God and evolution without mentioning the religious thinker who has probably thought more deeply about it than anyone else. Teilhard de Chardin (1881–1955) was a French Jesuit whose expertise in geology and paleontology led him to a life of reflection on the religious, and specifically Christian, meaning of evolution. For Teilhard evolution is not an obstacle to faith, but the most appropriate framework in which to articulate the meaning of faith.

Ordained a priest in 1911, Teilhard became a stretcher-bearer during World War I where his courage in battle led to a military medal and the Legion of Honor. Teilhard's most important work is *Le Phénomène humain* (1955; newly—and attractively—translated by Sarah Appleton-Weber as *The Human Phenomenon,* 1999). It was written during the twenties and thirties, but Teilhard's religious superiors forbade its publication until after his death. Because his ideas on faith and evolution were considered too novel at the time, he was sent to China where he participated energetically in geological expeditions and gained an excellent scientific reputation. But his scientific work only reinforced his awareness of the need to reinterpret Christianity in a post-Darwinian manner. He wrote volumes of essays on the topic of faith and evolution, but most of this material was published only posthumously.

After returning to France in 1946, Teilhard hoped to accept a teaching position at the Collège de Frances but his religious superiors, still alarmed at his ideas, refused permission. He then moved to the United States, continued his paleontological and archaeological work, and died largely unacknowledged in New York City on Easter Sunday, 1955.

Snubbed by his fellow Christians during his lifetime, Teilhard has arguably turned out to be the most important Christian thinker of the past century. Only time will assign him his proper place in the history of ideas, but to those who believe that religion must come to grips with evolution, Teilhard will forever be a heroic figure.

To those interested in pursuing his ideas, my own recommendation is to begin with collections of his essays, especially *The Future of Man* and *Activation of Energy,* rather than plunging immediately into *The Human Phenomenon.* Next to the latter, Teilhard's best known work is *The Divine Milieu,* a fertile interpretation of spirituality framed by an evolutionary sense of the world. For a lucid and blunt presentation of Teilhard's critique of classical theology's unpreparedness for evolution, see his book *Christianity and Evolution.* There are also many works available by critics of Teilhard, and certainly Teilhard would have welcomed such evaluations—if only he had been given the opportunity while still living. It is now left for others to refine, develop and apply his ideas to our contemporary situation.

94. What are Teilhard's main ideas on God and evolution?

We may sum them up, all too sketchily, as follows:

1. The whole universe is in evolution. Teilhard was one of the first scientists in the last century to recognize that the entire cosmos, and not just the stages of life and human existence, is a momentous process. Evolution has already brought forth the sphere of matter (the geosphere) and of life (the biosphere) on earth. It is now weaving something new on our planet—a sphere of "mind" (the noosphere).

2. There is a clear direction to the cosmic evolutionary story. In spite of the obvious, meandering "branching bush" character of life's evolution, the universe as a whole has clearly moved in the direction of increasing organized complexity. The process has passed through preatomic, atomic, molecular, unicellular, multicellular, vertebrate, primate phases and is now at work gathering the human mass toward a new future. During this journey it has manifested a measurable intensification of organized complexity. (Who can deny that the human brain is infinitely more complex in its organization than is an atom or a cell?) We can only wonder where cosmic evolution will now take its enduring tendency toward increasing complexity. But already we see complexification beginning to take place on a global scale. The modern world's emerging technologies, communication networks, educational and economic systems, and so forth, are bringing about a new kind of organized complexity. Teilhard did not live to see the internet, but his ideas clearly anticipated such developments.

3. During the course of evolution, consciousness has grown in direct proportion to the increase in organized physical complexity. Nature follows the "law of complexity-consciousness." Generally speaking, as matter has become more complex in its organization, consciousness—and in humans reflective self-consciousness—has also emerged. The "inside" of things has become more and more vivid, more centered and more free. And there is no reason to suspect that the law of complexity-consciousness, having reached the level of human consciousness, will now be suspended. If anything the earth, now at the level of the noosphere, appears to be moving in the direction of a global or planetary consciousness. Our planet and the universe as a whole are advancing toward integration at a new and higher level. Teilhard abstractly refers to the ultimate goal of this evolutionary process as "Omega," the final letter in the Greek alphabet. Religions identify it as God.

4. *God-Omega* is the ultimate end and explanation of evolution. Evolution happens because as God draws near to the world, the world is drawn into God. If we read beneath the surface of what science has discovered, we may understand the whole epic of evolution as a cosmic search for God. Our own religious aspirations, therefore, are an explicit blossoming and extension of the ageless cosmic search for its Center and Goal. It is through our religious longing that the entire universe now reaches out and opens itself, in different ways in diverse faith traditions, to its God. For Christians it is in Christ that the world is given the Center and Goal of its ongoing creation.

95. Where can I find a thorough systematic theological discussion of questions pertaining to God and evolution?

I have found considerable help in a contemporary version of Christian thought known as "process theology," and I have been using several of its main ideas in the preceding pages. I do not follow this theology in every respect, especially some of its ambiguous ideas about divine creation. But I am convinced that, on the whole, it deals with the troubling features of evolution more directly and competently than other theologies have.

Process theology reflects on God and nature in the light of ideas developed especially by the philosopher Alfred North Whitehead. This great thinker noted that all of nature, and not just life, is in process of becoming. To account for nature's restlessness, he insisted, we must postulate a principle that explains not only the order we observe in nature, but also the novelty that emerges each fresh moment of the world's becoming. The ultimate source of both the order and the novelty in evolution is "God."

God, according to process theology, is not interested simply in maintaining the status quo, but wants a universe that is always open to new creation. God, therefore, influences the cosmos by holding out before it, at every instant, new ways of becoming itself. God does not force the world into any rigid design, for such coercion would be incompatible with genuine love. Rather, God's power is persuasive. Power must have the quality of restraint if it is to coexist with love.

The world is in evolution, then, because God is a God of *persuasive* rather than coercive power. Unaware of evolution, traditional theology understood God almost exclusively as the source of order in nature and history. Process theology, however, finds this emphasis one-sided. The world is not just an order (what the Greeks called *cosmos*) but also a process; and what makes the world a process is that *new* forms of order are always being presented as possibilities for further becoming.

As the source of novelty, therefore, God is also the reason why the breakdown of present order often occurs—in the physical, biological, social, religious and political realms. Chaos, Whitehead says, is the "halfway house" between trivial forms of order and more interesting ones.

Evolution occurs because God is more interested in *adventure* than in preserving the status quo. By "adventure," process theology means the cosmic aim toward more intense versions of beauty, where "beauty" means the harmony of contrasts. In other words, God's will for the world is the maximization of beauty. God stimulates the world toward evolution so that deeper modes of beauty, along with beings that can enjoy beauty, will come into existence.

Process theology, to summarize, argues that the God of biblical religion is a God of persuasive love, the source of novelty and the stimulus to adventure. Unfortunately, Western theology has sometimes domesticated and frozen this "wild" adventurous deity into the orderly, decent, middle-class, gentlemanly God of the status quo. Evolution is important, then, for helping us recover a richer and more biblical sense of God.

96. Why, according to process theology, would God create a universe in which chance or randomness is allowed to exist along with order?

As to why the universe is intelligible enough for science to make sense of it, theology's response has always been that God is the ultimate source of order. Our awareness of evolution, however, requires an explanation of the nonorderly, random and chaotic aspects of the process. It is becoming increasingly apparent that the Creator does not want a universe that remains content with the way things are, but one that strives adventurously to become something more.

Reflecting on this new understanding of the universe, process theology can see a new meaning in the random occurrences which might otherwise seem utterly absurd. What evolutionary scientists vaguely refer to as random mutations and contingent, unpredictable events in natural history are characteristics we should expect in a universe that is unfinished and open to new creation. Without such deviant events the cosmos would long ago have become so rigidly locked into a fixed order that it would have remained lifeless and mindless. Order alone is not enough to have an interesting universe. You also need events that move the cosmos beyond any present state.

Process theology argues, then, that what we call random occurrences are essential in any universe that remains open to surprising, unpredictable outcomes in its future creation. Present instances of order must give way if the cosmos is to let in new forms of order, and we call those events that do not fit into our present sense of order "random." Such irregular events, however, are to be expected in any universe influenced by divine persuasive love. Our demand for a perfectly ordered universe is implicitly a demand that God be a coercive, dictatorial kind of power. Apparently God cannot be anything other than a love that respects the freedom and spontaneity of the other. This means there must be room for random events.

Certainly this also means that evolution will not be smooth and steady. On the other hand, a perfectly ordered world, one devoid of the messiness of contingent events, would be completely incompatible with a God who wills that the universe acquire increasing independence and become continually more open to new possibilities for becoming. Religious reflection on evolution should have no difficulty appropriating these ideas of process theology. Profession of belief in an infinite God's love of the finite world should lead us to expect that the universe will be open to the random events that let in the possibility of new creation.

97. Isn't Whitehead's notion of persuasive power a gratuitous diminishment of God's omnipotence?

Process theology would answer that it is not. For if "power" means "the capacity to influence," persuasive power has a much deeper impact on the world, at least in the final analysis, than would any hypothetically coercive exercise of force. A coercive kind of divine power, as we have already seen, would never allow the world to be something truly distinct from God. A world created by divine compulsion would be nothing more than an appendage to God's own being rather than a world unto itself.

Divine persuasion, on the other hand, offers possible ways for the world to emerge on its own. As I have often pointed out earlier, God allows the world to be somewhat self-creative. By not freezing the world into finished perfection through a single act of magicianship, God's persuasive power lets the world shape itself, even though God remains the creative source of all the possible paths the world could take. The point is, God does not push the universe down a narrow, predetermined trajectory, but gently and compassionately lures it toward ideal new forms of order.

The universe, however, does not always respond maximally to God's persuasion, especially when it reaches the human phase of its unfolding. The risk of evil remains and even intensifies with the emergence of human freedom. But, in the final analysis, persuasive power is more influential, more "powerful," than coercion. For the final product of God's persuasive love is a world that is much more substantial, free and self-actualizing than any imagined world passively produced by direct divine fabrication or design. We should have no trouble, therefore, thinking of God as omnipotent, provided we always understand power in a way consistent with divine love.

98. If God's power is persuasive rather than coercive, would this not make God somewhat detached from the world's evolution?

It might seem so at first. But a world that is allowed to find its own way, gently guided by the lure of new possibilities for self-actualization throughout the many millennia of evolution, ends up possessing much more distinctiveness, interior freedom and intensity of being than would any world emanating immediately out of a dictatorial deity's own will.

Moreover, as process theology emphasizes, the God of persuasive love is also a fully responsive God. God is so intimately related to the universe that every moment of its evolution is preserved eternally in God's own feeling and "memory." God experiences, suffers and "remembers" forever everything that occurs in the unfolding story of the universe. Thus God not only creates, but also saves or "redeems" the world from absolute perishing.

I do not want to give the impression that process thought is uncontroversial, but unlike many other kinds of theology it has the merit of boldly facing the harsh facts of evolution without unnecessarily softening them. And by embracing evolutionary science, it is able to conform all the more faithfully to the Christian image of God as suffering love. It allows us to view God's own loving self-restraint as a lure that invites the entire universe forward through time into a free and open future. The story of life told to us by evolutionary science fits into a grand adventure in which the universe is enticed, not forced, to make its way toward deeper freedom and the opportunity for more intimate relationship with God.

God's compassionate self-restraint allows for the world's self-creation and permits God to be much more deeply *related* to the world than a divine dictatorship would be. God's power may be said to be *relational* rather than unilateral. Relational power is more vulnerable, but ultimately more influential than unilateral power since it allows for more autonomy, integrity and richness in the world to which God is intimately related.

God acts powerfully in the world, moreover, by holding out to it a limitless range of possibilities which it may or may not follow. All the sufferings, struggles and achievements of evolution take place within God. And God's feeling of all the sufferings, struggles and achievements of nature and human history can, we may hope, serve to redeem and give meaning to all occurrences. Process theology emphasizes that God's compassion embraces the whole of creation, not just human history. All the billions of years of evolutionary travail and creativity are also in some way God's suffering and creativity. Nothing that occurs in creation takes place outside of God's compassionate feeling. Such a God is hardly "detached" from the world.

99. According to process theology, what is the purpose of this evolving universe?

For a process to be called purposeful it must be oriented toward the realization of a value. And so, in its aiming toward beauty, which has traditionally been seen as a "transcendental" value, the universe shows itself to be purposeful. What gives significance to evolution and to this whole universe-in-the-making is that the general orientation of cosmic process has been one of bringing about aesthetic intensity, a value that needs no justification beyond itself. Certainly there is more to cosmic purpose than this. But our universe can justifiably be called purposeful if it is oriented, at least in a general way, toward actualizing instances of beauty.

Today, in view of the reports we get from all of the sciences, there can be no serious doubt, at least when we take a long view of things, that the natural world has worked its way up from mere simplicity to vital complexity, from monotonous to more interesting versions of ordered novelty. Ours is a universe of emergent beauty. And even though this beauty is perishable, the fact that cosmic evolution has brought it about at all is enough to render suspect the confident modern claims that we live in a pointless universe.

We might even say that the universe is shaped by an "aesthetic cosmological principle." It is hard not to suspect that the universe has been lovingly "set up" from its beginning so as to allow for an ongoing process of emergent beauty, with all of the risk of tragedy and loss that aesthetic fragility entails. The renowned physicist Freeman Dyson has recently written that the universe follows a "principle of maximum diversity." By this he means that "the laws of nature and initial conditions are such as to make the universe as interesting as possible." On the basis of Whitehead's metaphysics we might broaden Dyson's happy intuition: the point of this evolving universe is to maximize beauty and, along with beauty, the possibility of subjective enjoyment. This is a world that can glorify and give joy to its Creator as well as to the many creatures in it.

100. What do the notions of "evil" and "sin" mean in process theology's interpretation of an evolutionary cosmos?

Evil and sin can no longer mean simply "disorder." In a static, preevolutionary conception of the universe evil might understandably have been defined as disorder. But in a world-in-the-making, evil also means anything that interferes with the world's ongoing evolution. Interestingly this may—at least in some contexts—include our human obsession with order or design.

In an evolving universe there are two forms of evil. There is the evil of disorder, examples of which are suffering, war, famine and death. But there is also the evil of monotony. The evil of monotony means clinging to trivial forms of order, refusing to open up to what is fresh and renewing even when it is relevant to do so. Because we realize that the embracing of novelty and diversity will disturb our present sense of order, we build walls around our cultural, political and economic lives so as to exclude what is new and different. Religion and theology may also become too obsessed with the tranquillity of order. Sometimes, therefore, it is only by risking the evil of chaos that we can avoid the evil of monotony.

We now realize that human life is interwoven with a world whose evolution is still occurring. One form of evil, therefore, takes the form of our decisions not to be part of the larger cosmic creation story. We may take our own restrictive sense of what constitutes good order and break our connections with the diversity that surrounds us as well as with the process that has produced us. Thinking of ourselves as the final end of cosmic creation, we may no longer feel the need to participate as one species among others in a complex earth-community. Or we may shape our civilized and religious lives in such a way as to exclude relevant social and economic diversity and novelty. In other words, we are tempted to the evil of monotony. Another name for this kind of evil is injustice.

Whatever else we may understand by "sin," in an evolving universe it means our refusal to participate in the ongoing creation and renewal of the cosmos. This understanding of sin implies that some of the attitudes and actions we formerly considered virtuous or holy, at a period of history when the universe seemed to be going nowhere, may now be exposed as the abetting of monotony. Our human tendency to absolutize a particular form of order may well be a refusal to allow new creation to occur.

Reflecting on the notions of sin and evil in the light of evolution allows us to recapture in a fresh way what the biblical prophets meant by justice and what Jesus meant by love. Justice and selfless love are ways in which evolution, once it has reached the level of human existence, avoids monotony and embraces adventure. Justice and love open us to what is truly different or "other," allowing our personal, social and political lives to be enriched and renewed.

101.   What is the purpose of our own lives in this evolving universe?

In responding to this final question let me appeal to the spirit of Whitehead, Teilhard and many others who have influenced my reflections on evolution. I have developed these points in much more depth in my book *God After Darwin: A Theology of Evolution,* and I can give only a very brief synopsis here.

The purpose of our own lives, when situated in the context of cosmic evolution, is to carry forward in whatever way we can the universe's general creative aim toward deeper and wider beauty. An "aesthetic" understanding of the evolving universe not only makes us ecologically more sensitive than we may have been before, but it also provides a robust foundation for ethical life in general.

In a post-Darwinian world our vocation, our mission in life, must be in some way to participate in the universe's own ageless labor of intensifying the reign of beauty. The evolving universe, as it turns out, is not indifferent to value, for it has always had an adventurous inclination to expand the dominion of beauty—to combine order with novelty, unity with multiplicity and harmony with contrast. And we may now integrate our own life-trajectories into the wider universe's habitual straining to actualize ever more intense versions of beauty.

Once we have become aware, with the help of evolutionary science, that our own lives and labors can add something new to the ongoing cosmic creation of beauty, our lives and deeds can gain a meaning only vaguely apprehended by the pre-Darwinian pictures of a static universe. A lively awareness of the general cosmic aim toward beauty gives us a rich context in which to cultivate the life of virtue. The virtues we idealize are still the traditional ones—humility, compassion, justice, gratitude, hope, and so on—the same ones that our great religious traditions have always taught. But now, in the context of evolution, we can see more clearly than ever that the good life is one that contributes meaningfully not only to the spiritual growth of the individual person, but also to the ongoing creation of a whole universe.

SELECTED READINGS

Denis Edwards, *The God of Evolution: A Trinitarian Theology* (Mahwah, N.J.: Paulist Press, 1999).

Jerry D. Korsmeyer, *Evolution and Eden: Balancing Original Sin and Contemporary Science* (Mahwah, N.J.: Paulist Press, 1998).

Langdon Gilkey, *Creationism on Trial: Evolution and God at Little Rock* (Charlottesville, Va.: University Press of Virginia, 1998).

John F. Haught, *God After Darwin: A Theology of Evolution* (Boulder, Colo.: Westview Press, 2000).

Kenneth Miller, *Finding Darwin's God* (New York: Harper & Row, 1999).

Ronald L. Numbers, *The Creationists* (New York: Knopf, 1992).

Keith Ward, *God, Chance and Necessity* (Oxford: Oneworld Press, 1996).

Richard Dawkins, *River Out of Eden* (New York: Basic Books, 1995).

Pierre Teilhard de Chardin, *Christianity and Evolution,* trans. by René Hague (New York: Harcourt Brace & Co., 1969).